Remote People

HIM HAILE SELASSIE THE FIRST KING
OF THE KINGS OF ETHIOPIA
(from the painting by a native artist)

EVELYN
WAUGH

Remote People

PENGUIN
CLASSICS

PENGUIN CLASSICS

Published by the Penguin Group
Penguin Books Ltd, 80 Strand, London WC 2R ORL, England
Penguin Group (USA) Inc., 375 Hudson Street, New York, New York 10014, USA
Penguin Group (Canada), 90 Eglinton Avenue East, Suite 700, Toronto, Ontario,
Canada M4P 2Y3 (a division of Pearson Penguin Canada Inc.)
Penguin Ireland, 25 St Stephen's Green, Dublin 2, Ireland (a division of Penguin Books Ltd)
Penguin Group (Australia), 250 Camberwell Road, Camberwell, Victoria 3124, Australia
(a division of Pearson Australia Group Pty Ltd)
Penguin Books India Pvt Ltd, 11 Community Centre, Panchsheel Park,
New Delhi – 110 017, India
Penguin Group (NZ), 67 Apollo Drive, Rosedale, Auckland 0632, New Zealand
(a division of Pearson New Zealand Ltd)
Penguin Books (South Africa) (Pty) Ltd, 24 Sturdee Avenue,
Rosebank, Johannesburg 2196, South Africa

Penguin Books Ltd, Registered Offices: 80 Strand, London WC 2R ORL, England

www.penguin.com

First published in Great Britain by Gerald Duckworth and Company Ltd 1931
First published in Penguin Books 1985
Published in Penguin Classics 2002
This edition published in Penguin Classics 2011

1

Copyright 1931 by Evelyn Waugh
All rights reserved

Set in 10.5/15pt Joanna MT Pro
Typeset by Jouve (UK), Milton Keynes
Text design by Claire Mason
Printed in Finland by Bookwell Ltd

A CIP catalogue record for this book is available from the British Library

ISBN: 978-0-141-19359-5

www.greenpenguin.co.uk

Contents

REMOTE PEOPLE

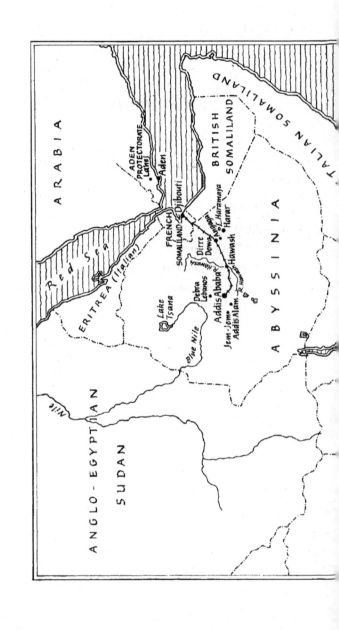

ARABIA

Red Sea

ADEN
PROTECTORATE
Lahej
•Aden

ERITREA (Italian)

FRENCH
SOMALILAND

Djibouti

BRITISH
SOMALILAND

ITALIAN SOMALILAND

Lake
Tsana

Debra
Lebanos

Blue Nile

Nile

Dirre
Dowa

•Haramaya
Harar

R. Hawash

Hawash

Addis Ababa

Jem-Jem
Addis Alam

ABYSSINIA

ANGLO - EGYPTIAN

SUDAN

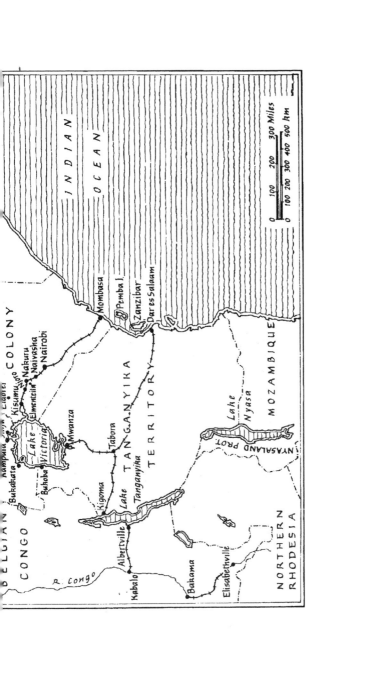

Remote People

ETHIOPIAN EMPIRE

ANTHROPOLOGIE

One

They were still dancing when, just before dawn on October 19th, 1930, the *Azay le Rideau* came into harbour at Djibouti. The band – a pitiably hot quartet in alpaca dinner-jackets – had long ago packed up their instruments and retired to their remote and stifling cabin. An Anamite boy was swabbing the deck and pushing into the scuppers sodden masses of paper streamers. Two or three stewards were at work pulling down the flags and festoons of coloured lights with which the ship had been decorated. One couple remained.

The girl was a second-class passenger to Mauritius; she was clearly of mixed blood, and she had chosen to wear the costume of a Tyrolean peasant, hired for the night from the ship's barber. Her partner was an officer in the French Foreign Legion; he wore an ill-fitting white uniform, open at the throat; he was quite young, blue-chinned, slightly pot-bellied, shorter than she by several inches. Their feet moved slowly over the wet boards to the music of a portable gramophone; at intervals they stopped, and unclasped each other, to rewind the instrument and reverse the single record.

For two days of gross heat the ship had been *en fête*. There had been deck-games, races for the children, a tombola with two-franc tickets and such prizes as could be procured on board – bottles of vermouth and eau-de-Cologne, tins of tobacco, sweets, lumps of coral, and ornamental cigarette-holders from Port Said. An autographed photograph of Marshal d'Esperez had been put up to auction and sold, amid wild applause, to a Press photographer for 900 francs; a cinema film had been exhibited by one of the passengers, with a faltering light on a screen that flapped restlessly in the hot breeze; there had been a horse-race decided by throw of dice, with a pari-mutuel and many hotly disputed results; at the deck bar there had been frequent orders for champagne, shared among families of French officials, six or eight of them to a bottle. Finally, on the last evening of the voyage, the fête had culminated in a fancy-dress dinner, a concert, and a ball.

It was a widely diverse company who had been thus indulged. There sat at my table a red-headed American on his way to Saigon, where he hoped to sell agricultural machinery; his watch-chain was loaded with Masonic insignia, he wore a ring of the interlaced initials of some other commercial secret society, he had Froth Blowers' cuff-links, and a Rotarian wheel in his buttonhole. No doubt he needed some such evidence of good-fellowship to aid his salesmanship, for he was unable to speak a word of French and was obliged to have the menu translated to him by his neighbour, the Italian proprietor of the third-best hotel in Madras. There was also an English girl who wore green sandals, and her mother who carried everywhere a small but assertive lapdog, which formed the basis of many complaints from those who were scandalised by her daughter's carmine toenails. There was a large number of French colonial officials, their wives and disorderly children, who make up the bulk of a normal Messageries Maritimes passenger list, on this occasion re-inforced by a draft of the Foreign Legion on their way to preserve discipline in Indo-China. The men travelled fourth class, sprawling about the lower deck by day, battened down in the hold at night. They were mostly Germans and Russians; in the evening they formed into little groups and sang songs. They had a band of drums and mouth-organs which came up to play in the first-class saloon on the evening of the con-cert. The drum was painted with the device 'Mon Jazz'. Two of them climbed through a port-hole one night in the Suez Canal and escaped. Next day a third tried to follow their example. We were all on deck drinking our morning apéri-tifs when we heard a splash and saw a shaven-headed figure in shirt-sleeves scrambling up the bank behind us. He had no hat and the sun was at its strongest. He ran through the sand, away from the ship, with gradually slackening speed. When he realised that no one was pursuing him he stopped and turned round. The ship went on. The last we saw of him was a figure stumbling after us and waving his arms. No one seemed the least put out by the occurrence. My cabin steward usually had some story to tell me of daily life on the lower deck. One day two of the legionaries began fighting and were put in the cells; another day a Chinaman went mad in the night and tried to commit suicide; another day there had been a theft on board, and so on. I think he used to invent a great deal to amuse me.

Besides this normal traffic of the line, there were about twenty of us bound for Djibouti on our way to Abyssinia for the emperor's coronation. My own presence there requires some explanation. Six weeks before, I had barely heard Ras Tafari's name. I was in Ireland, staying in a house where chinoiserie and Victorian Gothic contend for mastery over a Georgian structure. We were in the library, discussing over the atlas a journey I proposed to make to China and Japan. We began talking of other journeys, and so of Abyssinia. One of the party was on leave from Cairo; he knew something of Abyssinian politics and the coming coronation. Further information was contributed from less reliable sources; that the Abyssinian Church had canonised Pontius Pilate, and consecrated their bishops by spitting on their heads; that the real heir to the throne was hidden in the mountains, fettered with chains of solid gold; that the people lived on raw meat and mead; we looked up the royal family in the *Almanack de Gotha* and traced their descent from Solomon and the Queen of Sheba; we found a history which began: 'The first certain knowledge which we have of Ethiopian history is when Cush the son of — ascended the throne immediately after the Deluge'; an obsolete encyclopaedia informed us that, 'though nominally Christian, the Abyssinians are deplorably lax in their morals, polygamy and drunkenness being common even among the highest classes and in the monasteries'. Everything I heard added to the glamour of this astonishing country. A fortnight later I was back in London and had booked my passage to Djibouti. Two days later I was in a railway train going to Gloucestershire, where I met a friend who works on the staff of a London daily newspaper. I began boasting to him of my trip. My only anxiety was whether, as a tripper, I should be able to obtain access to the more inter-esting ceremonies. He said he thought that it might be arranged for me to go in some subordinate position to assist the paper. Accordingly, on my return from the week-end I saw his foreign editor and emerged from the interview for the first time in my life a fully accredited journalist, with a mini-ature passport authorising me to act as special correspondent during the ten days' coronation celebrations at Addis Ababa. Five days later I was on board the *Azay le Rideau* at Marseille, and ten days after that I was standing on deck in my pyjamas watching the dawn break over the low coastline of French Somaliland and over the haggard couple dancing to the gramophone.

Sleep had been impossible for some time, as the servants

of the Egyptian delegation had been at work assembling their masters' luggage immediately opposite the door of my cabin. Tin trunk after tin trunk was dragged out with loud military commands from the servant in charge and loud unmilitary remonstrances from his subordinates. It seemed hardly conceivable that five men could have so many clothes. And after the tin trunks came the great crates which contained the King of Egypt's present to the emperor. These had appeared on board at Port Said under escort of an armed patrol, and throughout the voyage had been guarded with some ostentation; their contents had been the object of wild speculation among the passengers, our imaginations wallowing in a profusion of biblical opulence – frankincense, sardonyx, madrepore, and porphyry. In point of fact, as appeared later, they contained a handsome but unexceptional suite of bedroom furniture.

There were three other delegations on board, from France, Holland, and Poland; a fourth, the Japanese, was awaiting our arrival at Djibouti. When not exchanging ceremonious introductions,[1] or pacing the decks at great speed, these

1. One of the first discoveries I made in my new profession was that nearly everyone in public life is obsessed by the fear that his name will be spelled wrong. As soon as it became known that I was a journalist – on board, and later at Addis Ababa – I was again and again approached by diffident officials tendering cards engraved with their names and correct titles.

envoys occupied themselves with finely emblazoned dispatch-cases, writing, typing and annotating their complimentary addresses.

At first sight there is something a little surprising in this sudden convergence on Abyssinia of the envoys of the civilised world, and I think that the Abyssinians were as surprised as anyone. After the sudden death of the Empress Zauditu in the spring of the year, immediately subsequent to the defeat of her husband Ras Gougsa, Ras Tafari notified the Powers that he proposed, as soon as he decently could, to assume the title of Emperor of Ethiopia, and included in this announcement, in the case of those few nations who maintained diplomatic representatives at his Court, an invitation to attend the ceremonies. A few years before, he had been crowned Negus; on that occasion his immediate neighbours had taken a few days' holiday to visit him, and there had been a mild exchange of courtesies by telegram. Something a little more conspicuous was expected of the imperial coronation, but the response of the world Powers exceeded Ethiopian expectation in a manner that was both gratifying and embarrassing. The states less directly interested in African affairs construed the notification as an invitation, and those with important local interests seized the opportunity for a display of cordiality and esteem out of all proportion to anything their previous relations with the country had given reason to expect. Two governments sent members of their royal families; the United States of America sent a gentleman of experience in the electric installation trade; the Governors of British Somaliland, the Soudan, Eritrea, the Resident at Aden, a marshal of France, an admiral, three airmen, and a marine band all appeared in various uniforms and orders. Substantial sums of public money were diverted to the purchase of suitable gifts; the Germans brought a signed photograph of General von Hindenburg and eight hundred bottles of Hock; the Greeks a modern bronze statuette; the Italians an aeroplane; the British a pair of elegant sceptres with an inscription composed, almost correctly, in Amharic.

Why all this fuss? Many people, even those intimately involved, were asking themselves this question. The simpler Abyssinians interpreted it as a suitable tribute to Abyssinian greatness; the kings of the world were doing homage. Others, a little more versed in world affairs, saw in it some plot against Abyssinian integrity – the *ferangi* had come to spy out the land. Honest colonists all over Africa grumbled at this absurd display of courtesy towards a mere native. At the legations themselves there was some restlessness; all this would still further complicate the task of impressing on the Abyssinians their real unimportance in the greater world; but what could they do? If some Powers chose to send dukes and princes, sceptres and aeroplanes, what could the others do but follow as best they could? Who started the stampede? And the Abyssinian Government may have wondered a little apprehensively how all these august gate-crashers were to be accommodated, and how the expenses of hospitality were to be met out of an irregular revenue and a depreciated currency. Why all this fuss?

One need not explore any deep political cause for a plausible explanation. Addis Ababa is not a place where great diplomatic reputations are easily won, the potentates of the Foreign Office do not keep any very keen scrutiny to see how their cadets are shaping in that rare altitude. Diplomatic appointments there may be a suitable reward for an industrious consul-general, but it is scarcely the foundation of a career. Who could blame these officials if occasionally there crept into their dispatches phrases tending to estimate with some generosity the importance of the land of their exile? Is Abyssinia not the source of the Blue Nile? May there not be vast mineral wealth in those unprospected hills? And if, in the trivial course of compound life, that unvarying round of modest entertainment, there suddenly came to the women of the diplomatic corps – poor half-sisters of the great ladies of Washington or Rome – the possibility of sudden splendour, of royalty and gold braid, curtseys and champagne and handsome ADCs, who can blame them if they strengthened their menfolk in urging the importance of really imposing special representation at the festivities?

And need one wonder if states very remote from Africa – sledded Polaks and blond Swedes – decided to join in the party? If the glamour of Abyssinia had drawn me there from a life of comparative variety and freedom, why not them from their grey chanceries? Gun-cases among their trunks of uniform showed that they intended to make the most of their jaunt, and several of them, I know, had paid their own fares. 'Nous avons quatre citoyens ici, mais deux sont juifs,' one attaché explained to me, and proceeded to demonstrate the apparatus with which, during his sojourn in Africa, he hoped to add to his already extensive collection of butterflies.

Day broadened rapidly and the dancers finally separated and went off to bed. Lighters came out from shore and coaling began. Planks stretched between the ship and the barges. One of them broke, throwing the Somali coolies heavily on to the coal – a drop of ten feet or more. One lay on his back groaning after the others had got up. The foreman threw a lump of coal at him. He groaned and turned on to his face; another lump, and he staggered to his feet and resumed work. Somali boys came swimming round the ship calling for money to be thrown them. Passengers appeared on deck.

We lay well out in the bay. Between us and the landing-stage lay the wreck of a large cargo boat, heeled over on her side, swept clear, and corroded by the tide. She is mentioned in Armandy's *La Désagréable Partie de Campagne*.

Soon it began to rain.

Great uncertainty prevailed as to how or when we should

get to Addis Ababa. The purser had been most reassuring. He had wired to the station informing them of the number of passengers, he said. A special train would be ready for us that day. There were conflicting rumours about, however. Those who had some previous acquaintance with Abyssinia remarked that things could not conceivably be as smooth as that. Report circulated that there was to be a special train, but that it was only for the delegations; a further report that there were to be two trains, one that morning for delegations, one in the evening for unofficial passengers; that a shipload of passengers were arriving that day from Aden from a P. & O. liner, and that there was very little hope of accommodation; that all unofficial traffic had been stopped until after the coronation. The delegations themselves knew nothing of their arrangements except that they were expected to luncheon at the governor's house.

We waited our turn to go ashore with some anxiety. The coolies droned dismally up and down the unstable planks; the little boys in the water cried for francs, or appeared shivering on deck, offering to amuse us by jumping back again; guns on shore boomed the salutes as the Government launch fetched each delegation in turn. The warm rain poured down steadily.

Eventually we were free to land. There was another Englishman travelling to Addis Ababa, an elderly gentleman on his way to the legation as a private visitor. Throughout the voyage he had studied a formidable little book about tropical hygiene, and passed on to me much disquieting information about malaria and blackwater, cholera and elephantiasis; he used, over his cigar in the evenings, to explain how hook-worms ate their way from the soles of the feet to the internal organs, how jiggers laid their eggs under the toenails, and retailed the symptoms of slow paralysis with which the spirillum tick might infect us.

Together we put our luggage in charge of the French-speaking native porter of the Hôtel des Arcades and went to the English vice-consul – an amiable young shipping-clerk – who told us that there were in fact two trains that evening, but both of them were reserved for delegations; the next train was three days later; that was reserved for the Duke of Gloucester; there was another one three days after that – reserved for Prince Udine. He could hold out very little hope of our getting up to Addis, but he would see what could be done. In a state of mind born of this information we drove to the Hôtel des Arcades. Our topis were soft on our heads, our white suits clinging about our shoulders. The porter said I must go with him to the customs. We arrived there to find a damp native soldier on guard with water running down his rifle. The customs officer was at the reception at Govern-ment House, he said. He could not tell what time he would return or whether he would return at all that day. By means of the hotel porter I pointed out that we must have our luggage to change into dry clothes. Nothing could be moved until the officer returned, he said. The porter, without more ado, picked up the nearest pieces and began piling them into the taxi. The guard remonstrated, but the porter continued undeterred. Then we drove back to the hotel.

This was a two-storeyed building with an arcaded front of shabby stucco; at the back a wooden staircase led to two broad verandahs on to which the two or three bedrooms opened. There was a lemon-tree in the yard inhabited by a misanthropic black monkey. The proprietress was a handsome Frenchwoman abounding in commercial good nature. She gave us warm water and a room to change in, and made light of our troubles. It was her peculiar fortune to subsist upon the inadequacies of the Franco-Ethiopian railway service, for no one voluntarily spends long in Djibouti.

This fact, sufficiently clear from our earliest impression, became clearer when, after luncheon, the rain having stopped, we drove for a tour of the town. We bumped and rocked along in a one-horse cab through pools of steaming mud. The streets, described by the official guide book as 'elegant and smiling', were mere stretches of wasteland between blocks of houses. These, in the European quarter, were mostly built on the same plan as the hotel, arcaded and decaying.

'They look as though they might fall down any minute,' remarked my companion as we drove past one more than usually dissolute block of offices, and while we looked they actually did begin to fall. Great flakes of stucco crumbled from the front; a brick or two, toppling from the coping, splashed into the mud below. Some scared Indian clerks scampered into the open, a Greek in shirt-sleeves appeared from the house opposite, a group of half-naked natives rose from their haunches and, still scouring their teeth with sticks of wood, gazed apprehensively about them. Our driver pointed excitedly with his whip and admonished us in Somali. It had been an earthquake which, in the more sensible motion of the cab, had escaped our notice.

We jolted on past a whitewashed mosque to the camel-market and native quarter. The Somalis are a race of exceptional beauty, very slender and erect, with delicate features and fine, wide-set eyes. Most of them wore a strip of rag around their waists, and a few coils of copper wire on wrists and ankles. Their heads were either shaven or dyed with ochre. Eight or nine harlots besieged our carriage until whipped away by the driver; innumerable naked children splashed through the mud after us, screaming for baksheesh. Some splendid fellows with spears, in from the country, spat contemptuously as we passed. We came to the outskirts of the town, where the huts, formerly grass-thatched, mud-built squares, became little domed structures like inverted birds' nests, made out of twigs, grass, rags, and flattened tins, with one hole through which a man might crawl on his belly. We returned by the sea front past a few fairly ordered goods yards and corrugated-iron sheds. I stopped at the post office and conscientiously cabled back to my employers the arrival of the various delegations. When I returned to the hotel I found the vice-consul there with the good news that he had obtained a carriage for us in the first special train that evening. Elated though we felt, the heat was still overpowering; we went to sleep.

At evening, with the knowledge of our imminent departure, Djibouti suddenly became more tolerable. We visited the shops, bought a French novel with an inflammatory wrapper, some Burma cheroots, and changed some money, getting, in return for our tattered and grimy notes of the Banque d'Indo-Chine, massive silver dollars of superb design.[1]

1. The Marie Thérèse thaler, ousted elsewhere in Africa by the meagre rupee or the sordid East African shilling, is still the basic coin of Abyssinia. It is not the most commodious form of currency. It varies in value with the price of silver, and gives opportunity for a great deal of rather shady speculation. Notes are issued by the Bank of Abyssinia against a silver deposit. Even at Dirre-Dowa, two stations down the line from Addis, the local branch of the bank charges a three per cent discount in cashing them, and except in the capital or on the railway they are quite valueless. I saw a small caravan setting out for three months in the interior which carried two mule-loads of dollars for current expenses. It is the coin which the people are used to, and they insist on having it. The Menelik dollar went out of circulation because no one wanted it. The half and quarter dollar are accepted after prolonged scrutiny. There are two issues, in one of which the lion's tail is straight, while in the other it curls back at the

Most recent books about Abyssinia – and I had read many between West Meath and Marseille – contain graphic descriptions of the train journey between Djibouti and Addis Ababa. Normally there is a weekly service which does the journey in three days; the two nights are spent in hotels at Dirre-Dowa and Hawash. There are several good reasons for not travelling at night; one is that the lights in the train are liable to frequent failure; another that during the rainy season it is not unusual for parts of the line to get washed away; another that the Galla and Danakil, through whose country the line passes, are still primarily homicidal in their interests, and in the early days of the railway formed a habit, not yet wholly eradicated, of taking up steel sleepers here and there to forge into spear-heads.[1] During coronation week, however, it was found necessary, if the rolling-stock was to

tip; both are of equally pure silver, but the second is usually refused, even as a tip. A hundred years ago the Marie Thérèse thaler was the coin of the Arab trader from Tangier to Manchuria. Now its general use survives only in Arabia and Ethiopia. It is still minted in Vienna from the 1780 die, a gracious survival which forms, however, a very deceptive introduction to Ethiopian manners.

1. There are also frequent raids on the telegraph wires, pieces of which are much valued as bangles and bracelets. Shortly before the coronation, for the convenience of the Press, the Government seized a number of men who may have been implicated in the business, cut off a hand and a foot apiece, and exhibited them, one at each halt down the line. No doubt the example was salutary, but the telegraph service remained very irregular.

be adequate to the additional traffic, to run through trains. We left Djibouti after dinner on Friday and arrived at Addis on Sunday morning. There was, of course, no restaurant car and the few wagon-lits were occupied by the delegations, but my companion and I had each the side of a first-class carriage to ourselves; we stopped for meals at wayside buffets; it was a fairly comfortable journey.

We passed in the darkness the intolerable desolation of French Somaliland – a country of dust and boulders, utterly devoid of any sign of life, and arrived at Dirre-Dowa at dawn. This orderly little township sprang up during the construction of the railway on the land conceded to the French company, and has lived on the railway ever since with slightly diminishing prosperity. It contains two hotels, a café, and a billiard-saloon, a few shops and offices, a bank, a flour-mill, one or two villas, and the residence of an Abyssinian governor. Bougainvillaea and acacia-trees border the streets. Twice a week the arrival of a train stirs up a few hours' activity; travellers arrive for the hotels; luggage is carried about the street; postal officials sort out the mail; commercial agents put on their sun-helmets and saunter down with their invoices to the goods office; then, like a small island when the mail-boat steams out of harbour, Dirre-Dowa relapses into its large siesta.

This, however, was no ordinary week. Not since 1916 – the civil war before the last – when Lej Yasu's Mohammedan followers were massacred just over the hills at Harar – had Dirre-Dowa known so many radically disturbing events as this succession of special trains bringing the emperor's visitors to the coronation. Flagstaffs painted with the Abyssinian colours had been planted down the main streets, and lines of yellow, red, and green flags strung between them; motor cars had been brought by train from the capital – for there are no roads outside the town – to convey the delegates to breakfast; the irregular troops of the whole province had been mobilised to line the way.

It was a grand and startling spectacle. My companion and I waited behind for some minutes in our carriage until the formal greetings were at an end and the delegates were clear of the station. Then we crossed the platform into the square. It was quite empty and quite silent. On three sides stood the Abyssinian soldiers; in front, where the main avenue led up to the governor's house, the last of the cars was just disappearing; as far as one could see stood the ranks of motionless, white-clothed tribesmen, bareheaded, barefooted, with guns on their shoulders; some had olive skins and keen aquiline features; others were darker, with thick lips and flat noses showing the infection of slave blood; most of them were of good height and strong physique; all wore curly black beards. Their dress was the invariable costume of the country – a long white shirt, white linen breeches loose above the knee and tight at the calves like jodhpurs, and the *chamma*, a white shawl worn like the toga over one shoulder, and a bandoleer of cartridges prominently displayed. In front of each section stood their chief in the gala dress so frequently photographed for the European Press. This, varying in grandeur with the wearer's wealth, consisted of a head-dress of lion's mane and gold ornament, a lion's skin, a brilliantly striped shirt, and a long sword curving out behind for some three feet or more; in some cases the lion's skin was represented by a garment of embroidered satin, like a chasuble, slit in front and behind in conventionalised tail and legs. It was a memorable experience to emerge, after the Latin holiday-making on the *Azay le Rideau*, the scramble at Djibouti, and the unquiet night in the train, into the sweet early morning air and the peace cast by these motionless warriors; they seemed at once so savage and so docile; great shaggy dogs of uncertain temper held for the moment firmly at leash.

We breakfasted at the hotel, and smoked a pipe on the terrace, awaiting the return of the delegates. Presently the soldiers who had been squatting on their haunches were called to attention; the cars came down the hill bearing diplomats handsomely refreshed by a banquet of porridge, kippers, eggs, and champagne. We returned to the train and resumed our journey.

From now until Hawash, where we arrived at sundown, the line ran through mile upon mile of featureless bush country – thorn, scrub, and flat, brownish mimosa-trees, and dust, ant-hills, a few vultures, now and then a dry water-course or outcrop of stone, nothing else, hour upon hour. At intervals we stopped for water at stations consisting of a single shed and barbed-wire compound; here there was always a guard drawn up to meet us, two or three uniformed railway police and the local chief with his levy of sometimes a dozen, sometimes fifty, men. At noon we lunched in a tent at a halt named Afdem; luncheon consisted of four courses of meat variously prepared. We waited four hours at Hawash, from six until ten, while mechanics experimented with the lighting of the train; an armed guard squatted at the door of each coach. There are several sheds at Hawash, two or three bungalows of railway officials, a concrete platform, and an inn. After dinner we sat in the yard of the inn on hard little chairs, or paced about the platform or stumbled between the steel sleepers of the permanent way; there was no village or street; it was better to keep in the open as there were fewer mosquitoes; the lights in the carriage windows flashed fever-ishly on and off. Presently a group of ragged Gallas appeared and began to dance; two performed in the centre of the cir-cle; the others stood round singing, stamping their feet and clapping their hands; they acted a lion hunt in dumb show. The guards wanted to drive them away, but the Egyptian Minister restrained them and gave a handful of dollars to the dancers; this set them going more eagerly and they spun about in the dust like tops; they were extremely fierce men, their long hair matted with butter and mud, and their thin, black bodies hung with scraps of skin and sacking.

At last the lighting was put right and we started again. Hawash lies at the foot of the highlands; throughout the night we climbed steadily. Each time we were jolted into consciousness between intermittent periods of sleep, we found the air fresher and the temperature lower, and by early morning we had wrapped ourselves in rugs and overcoats. We breakfasted before dawn at a place called Mojo and resumed our journey just as the first light began to break. It revealed a profound change in the landscape; the bush and plain had disappeared, and in its place there extended crests of undulating downland with a horizon of blue mountains. Wherever one looked were rich little farms, groups of circular thatched huts inside high stockades, herds of fine humped cattle browsing in deep pastures, fields of corn and maize being worked by families; camel caravans swayed along the track by the railway, carrying fodder and fuel. The line still mounted, and presently, between nine and ten, we came in sight, far ahead of us, of the eucalyptus-woods that surround Addis Ababa. Here, at a station named Akaki, where an Indian merchant maintains a great warehouse and a ras had constructed a great part of what was to be an hotel, we stopped again to allow the delegates time to shave and put on their uniforms. Tin trunks and dressing-cases appeared again, valets ran between the luggage-van and the sleeping-cars. The Dutch Minister soon appeared at the side of the line in cocked hat and gold braid, the Egyptian in *tarboosh* and epaulettes, the Japanese in evening coats and white waistcoats and top hats; the chiefs inspected their subordinates; then all got into the train again and proceeded. We puffed up the winding track for another half-hour and at last arrived at Addis Ababa.

The station is a large, two-storeyed, concrete building with a single covered platform. Red carpet had been put out, and before the carpet were drawn up a very different body of troops from those we had passed on the way. These were squat, coal-black boys from the Soudanese border. They wore brand-new, well-cut, khaki uniforms; the lion of Judah shone in polished brass on cap badges and buttons; with bayonets fixed and rifles of recent pattern. Beside them a band of bugle and drums, with a little black drummer pois-ing crossed sticks above the big drum. But for the bare feet below their puttees, they might have been the prize platoon of some Public School OTC. In front of them with drawn sword stood a European officer. This was a squad of Tafari's own guard. Hardly had the blood congealed on Gougsa's mangled corpse, or the bereaved empress succumbed to her sudden chill, before orders had been issued for the for-mation of this corps. Officers had come from Belgium to undertake the training. The men had been recruited from Tafari's own scattered provinces, bound to the throne by direct feudal allegiance. In six months he had trained a regiment of them – the nucleus of an organised national army.

As the train stopped, the guard presented arms; the head chamberlain advanced in a blue satin cloak to greet the delegations, and the band struck up. This, too, was an innovation. It is my misfortune to be quite insensible to music, but I was told by all who heard them that the tunes played as each delegation was received were, in practically all cases, easily recognisable. One thing I did realise, and that was their unusual length; there was no skimping of difficulties, every anthem was played through thoroughly verse by verse. The Poles came out easy winners in prolixity. Finally the Ethiopian anthem was played; we heard this so often during the next ten days that it became vaguely familiar, even to me. (It began like the Hymn 'Lights above celestial Salem', but ended quite differently.)

Eventually the last delegation disappears. The Minister's daughters have come from the British Legation to meet the train. They ask me what arrangements have been made for my accommodation, and I reply, to the best of my knowledge, none. Consternation. They say that the town is completely full. It will be impossible to get a room now. It is possible there may be a tent somewhere at the legation; it is conceivable that one of the hotels will let me pitch it in the yard. We get into the car and mount the hill into the town. Half-way up we pass the Hôtel de France. At the entrance stands the supremely Western figure of Irene Ravensdale in riding habit. We stop to greet her. I run indoors and ask the manager whether there is, by any chance, a vacant room. Why, yes, certainly. It is not a very good room, it is in an outhouse behind the hotel; but, if I care to take it, it is mine for two pounds a day. I accept eagerly, sign the register, and rejoin Irene. The legation car and the luggage has disappeared. Instead, the street is full of Abyssinians arriving from the country on mules, slaves trotting all round them, clearing and obstructing the way. We return to the hotel, lunch, and go to sleep. Later the luggage turns up in the charge of a good-hearted young Englishman, who, having failed as a coffee farmer, has been engaged temporarily at the legation as general help. The preposterous *Alice in Wonderland* fortnight has begun.

Two

In fact, it is to *Alice in Wonderland* that my thoughts recur in seeking some historical parallel for life in Addis Ababa. There are others: Israel in the time of Saul, the Scotland of Shakespeare's *Macbeth*, the Sublime Porte as one sees it revealed in the dispatches of the late eighteenth century, but it is in *Alice* only that one finds the peculiar flavour of galvanised and translated reality, where animals carry watches in their waistcoat pockets, royalty paces the croquet lawn beside the chief executioner, and litigation ends in a flutter of playing-cards. How to recapture, how retail, the crazy enchantment of these Ethiopian days?

First let me attempt to convey some idea of the setting. Addis Ababa is a new town; so new, indeed, that not a single piece of it appears to be really finished. Menelik the Great chose the site forty years ago and named it, when it was still a hillside encampment, 'The New Flower'. Till then the Government had shifted between the ancient, priest-ridden cities of the north, mobile according to the exigencies of fuel, but morally centred on Axum, the ecclesiastical capital, as the French monarchy centred on Rheims. Menelik was the first king to break the tradition of coronation at Axum, and at the time even his vast military prestige suffered from the breach. It is mentioned by contemporary writers as a source of weakness; actually it was a necessary part of his policy. He was no longer merely king of the Christian, Amharic highlanders, he was emperor of a great territory embracing in the west the black pagan Shankallas, in the east the nomad anthropophagous Danakils, in the south-east the Ogaden Desert inhabited by Somalis, and in the south the great belt of cultivable land held by the Mohammedan Gallas. At Addis Ababa he found the new centre for his possessions, still in the highlands among his own people, but on their extreme edge; immediately at its foot lies the territory of the wretched Guraghi, the despised, ill-conditioned people who provide the labour for building and sweeping; Hawash is the land of the Gallas. Addis Ababa is the strategic point for the control of these discordant dominions. Lej Yasu contemplated a further, more radical change. It appears to have been his purpose, or the purpose of his counsellors, to reorientate the empire from Harar and build up a great Mohammedan Power, which should, in the event of the victory of the Central Powers in Europe, enclose the whole Somali coastline. It was an intemperate ambition which needed no European intervention to encompass its downfall. The exact circumstances of his failure may, perhaps, never be known, nor the extent to which these plans were even clearly formulated. It is certain that he was in correspondence with the Mad Mullah in British Somaliland. It is widely believed that he had in his last years frankly apostatised from the Church; his father's Mohammedan origin added colour to this report, and proof was supplied in the form of his portrait wearing a turban which purported to have been taken at Harar. Many, however, declare that this conclusive piece of evidence was fabricated in Addis Ababa by an Armenian photographer. Whatever the truth of these details, the fact is clear that the unfortunate young man fell, not, as is usually said, through his grosser habits of life, which, indeed, tended rather to endear him to his humbler subjects, but through his neglect of what must remain for many years to come the strength of the Ethiopian Empire – its faith and the warlike qualities of the Amharic hillsmen. Lej Yasu has not been seen since 1916. He is said to be living, listless and morbidly obese, under Ras Kassa's guardianship at Fiche, but a traveller who lately passed the reputed house of his captivity remarked that the roof was out of repair and the entrance overgrown with weeds. People do not readily speak of him, for the whole country is policed with spies, but more than one European who enjoyed the confidence of his servants told me that the name is still greatly respected among the lower orders. He has, through his mother, the true blood of Menelik. They describe him as a burly young man with compelling eyes, recklessly generous and superbly dissipated. Tafari's astute diplomacy strikes some of them as far less kingly.

There was no constitution in Ethiopia. The succession was determined in theory by royal proclamation, in practice by bloodshed. Menelik had left no male and no legitimate children. Lej Yasu's mother was his daughter and he had nominated Lej Yasu. In the circumstances, Lej Yasu had named no successor and there was thus no indisputable heir. By right of Menelik's blood, his second daughter reigned as the Empress Zauditu, but her religious duties occupied more of her attention than the routine of government. A regent was necessary; three or four noblemen had, by descent, equal claims to the office. The most important of these was Ras Kassa, but deeply concerned with religion and the management of his estates, he was unambitious of wider obligations. The danger which confronted the country was that Menelik's conquests would again disintegrate into a handful of small kingdoms, and that the imperial throne would become a vague overlordship. In such a condition, Abyssinian independence could scarcely hope to survive the penetration of European commercial interests. The rases appreciated the position and realised that there was only one man whose rank, education, intellect, and ambition qualified him for the throne. This was Ras Tafari. Accordingly, by their consent and choice, he became Negus. With the general public, outside his own provinces, his prestige was slight; he was distinguished neither by the blood of Menelik nor any ostentatious feat of arms. Among the rases he was *primus inter pares*;

one of themselves chosen to do a job, and answerable to them for its satisfactory execution. From this precarious position in the years that followed, Tafari gradually built up and consolidated his supremacy. He travelled in Europe; he was at pains to impress visiting Europeans with his enlightenment. He played on the rivalries of the French and Italian representatives, and secured his own position at home by advancing his country's position in the world. He obtained admission to the League of Nations; everywhere he identified himself with his country, until Europe came to look to him as its natural ruler.

Even so, he had to fight for his throne. In the spring of 1930 a powerful noble named Ras Gougsa[1] rebelled. He was the husband of the empress; they had been divorced, but maintained cordial and intimate relations. Tafari's army was victorious, and, in the blood-thirsty rout, Gougsa was himself slain. The empress died suddenly next day, and Tafari, with the assent of the rases, proclaimed himself emperor, fixing for his coronation the earliest date by which preparations could adequately be made. The coronation festivities were thus the final move in a long and well-planned strategy. Still maintaining his double ruff of trumping at home with prestige abroad, abroad with his prestige at home, Tafari had

1. There is a Ras Gougsa, quite unconnected with the rebel, who is still living. He acted as host to the American delegation during the coronation.

two main motives behind the display. He wished to impress on his European visitors that Ethiopia was no mere agglomeration of barbarous tribes open to foreign exploitation, but a powerful, organised, modern state. He wanted to impress on his own countrymen that he was no paramount chief of a dozen independent communities, but an absolute monarch recognised on equal terms by the monarchies and governments of the great world. And if, in the minds of any of his simpler subjects, courtesy and homage became at all confused, if the impression given was that these braided delegates (out for a holiday from their serious duties, an unusual pageant, and perhaps a few days' shooting) had come in their ruler's name to pay tribute to Ethiopian supremacy – so much the better. The dismembered prisoners of Adowa were still unavenged. The disconcertingly eager response of the civilised Powers gave good colour to this pretension. 'We did not think so much of Tafari,' remarked the servant of one Englishman, 'until we learned that your king was sending his own son to the coronation'; and there can be no doubt that the other rases, confronted at close quarters with the full flood of European diplomacy, realised more clearly that other qualities were needed for the government of a modern state than large personal property and descent from Solomon. This very exuberance, however, of European interest tended to hinder the accomplishment of the emperor's first ambition. The gun-cases were his undoing,

for in the days that followed the celebrations, when the delegations were scattered on safari about the interior of the
country, they had the opportunity of observing more than
had been officially prepared for them. They saw just how far
the emperor's word ran in the more distant parts of his
dominions; they saw the frail lines of communication which
bound the Government to its outposts; they saw something
of the real character of the people, and realised how inadequate an introduction to the national life were the caviare
and sweet champagne of Addis Ababa.

I have said above that the coronation was fixed for the earliest date by which preparations could be made. This statement needs some qualification and brings me back from this
political digression to the description of Addis Ababa with
which I began the chapter, for the first, obvious, inescapable
impression was that nothing was ready or could possibly be
made ready in time for the official opening of the celebrations six days hence. It was not that one here and there
observed traces of imperfect completion, occasional scaf-
folding or patches of unset concrete; the whole town seemed
still in a rudimentary stage of construction. At every corner
were half-finished buildings; some had been already abandoned; on others, gangs of ragged Guraghi were at work. It is
difficult to convey in words any real idea of the inefficiency
to which low diet and ill-will had reduced these labourers.

One afternoon I watched a number of them, twenty or thirty in all, under the surveillance of an Armenian contractor, at work clearing away the heaps of rubble and stone which encumbered the courtyard before the main door of the palace. The stuff had to be packed into wooden boxes swung between two poles, and emptied on a pile fifty yards away. Two men carried each load, which must have weighed very little more than an ordinary hod of bricks. A foreman circulated among them, carrying a long cane. When he was engaged elsewhere the work stopped altogether. The men did not sit down, chat, or relax in any way; they simply stood stock-still where they were, motionless as cows in a field, sometimes arrested with one small stone in their hands. When the foreman turned his attention towards them they began to move again, very deliberately, like figures in a slow-motion film; when he beat them they did not look round or remonstrate, but quickened their movements just perceptibly; when the blows ceased they lapsed into their original pace until the foreman's back being turned, they again stopped completely. (I wondered whether the Pyramids were built in this way.) Work of this nature was in progress in every street and square of the town.

Addis Ababa extends five or six miles in diameter. It lies at a height of eight thousand feet, with a circle of larger hills to the north of it, culminating at Entoto in a mountain of about ten thousand. The station is at the southern extremity of the town, and from it a broad road leads up to the post office and principal commercial buildings. Two deep watercourses traverse the town, and round their slopes, and in small groves of eucalyptus scattered between the more permanent buildings, lie little clusters of *tukals*, round native huts, thatched and windowless. Down the centre of the main thoroughfares run metalled tracks for motor-traffic, bordered on either side by dust and loose stones for mules and pedestrians; at frequent intervals are sentry-boxes of corrugated iron, inhabited by drowsy, armed policemen; there are also police at point duty, better trained than most of the motor-drivers in European signals of control. Attempts are even made, with canes and vigorous exchanges of abuse, to regulate the foot-traffic, a fad which proves wholly unintelligible to the inhabitants. The usual way for an Abyssinian gentleman to travel is straight down the middle of the road on mule-back with ten or twenty armed retainers trotting all round him; there are continual conflicts between the town police and the followers of the country gentleman, from which the police often come out the worse.

Every man in Abyssinia carries arms; that is to say, he wears a dagger and bandoleer of cartridges round his waist and has a slave-boy walking behind with a rifle. There is some question about the efficacy of these weapons, which are mostly of some antiquity. Some are of the Martini type, probably salvaged from the field of Adowa, others are comparatively modern, bolt-action weapons and old, English service-rifles. They have percolated through singly from Somaliland and been brought in, disguised as other merchandise, by such romantic gun-runners as Arthur Rimbaud and M. de Mont-fried. Cartridges are a symbol of wealth and, in the interior, a recognised medium of exchange; their propriety for any particular brand of firearm is a matter of secondary import-ance; often the brass ammunition displayed in the bandoleers will not fit the rifle carried behind, and there is usually a large percentage of expended cartridges among it.

The streets are always a lively scene; the universal white costume being here and there relieved by the brilliant blues and violets of mourning or the cloaks of the upper classes. The men walk about hand in hand in pairs and little groups; quite often they are supporting some insensible drunkard. Women appear in the markets, but take no part in the gen-eral street-lounging of their men. Occasionally a woman of high degree passes on a mule; under a vast felt hat her face is completely bandaged over with white silk, so that only the two eyes appear, like those of a hooded rider of the Ku Klux Klan. There are numerous priests, distinguished by long gowns and high turbans. Sometimes the emperor passes in a great red car surrounded by cantering lancers. A page sits behind holding over his head an umbrella of crim-son silk embroidered with sequins and gold tassels. A guard sits in front nursing a machine-gun under a plush shawl; the chauffeur is a European wearing powder-blue livery and the star of Ethiopia.

There are open fields immediately round the station, broken on one side by the thin roof of the public baths, where a spring wells up scalding hot. It is from here that the water is conveyed in petrol-cans for our baths at the hotel. On the other side of the road stands the execution shed. Public hanging has recently been abolished in Tafari's own provinces, and the gibbet-tree before the cathedral cut down to make room for a little (unfinished) garden and a statue of Menelik. Homicides are now shot behind closed doors, though the bereaved relatives still retain the right of carrying out the sentence. No distinction is made in Abyssinian law between manslaughter and murder; both are treated as offences against the family of the dead man. It is for them to choose whether they will take blood-money or blood; the price varies with the social status of the deceased, but is usually about a thousand dollars (£70 or £80). Occasionally the murderer prefers to die rather than pay. There was a case in Addis Ababa shortly before our arrival in which the bargaining was continued in the execution shed right up to the firing of the shot; the relatives abating their price dollar by dollar, the murderer steadfastly refusing to deprive his children of their full inheritance.

As part of the general policy for tidying up the town for the arrival of the visitors, high stockades have been erected, or are being erected, down all the streets, screening from possibly critical eyes the homes of the poorer inhabitants. Half-way up the hill stands the Hôtel de France, a place of primitive but cordial hospitality, kept by a young Frenchman and his wife who have seen better days as traders in hides and coffee at Djibouti. At the top of the hill, in front of the post office, two main roads branch out to right and left, the one leading to the Gebbi (Tafari's palace), the other to the native bazaar and Indian quarter. Work is in progress at the crossroads making a paved and balustraded island round a concrete cenotaph which is destined to commemorate the late empress. A fourth road leads obliquely to Gorgis, the cathedral of St George.

The buildings are mostly of concrete and corrugated iron. There is another large hotel kept by a Greek, the Imperial, most of which has been requisitioned for the Egyptian delegation. There are two or three small hotels, cafés, and bars, kept either by Greeks or Armenians. There is another large hotel under construction. It was being made specially for the coronation, but is still hopelessly unready. It is here that the Marine band of HMS *Effingham* are put up. A nightclub advertises that it will open shortly with a cabaret straight from the Winter Garden Theatre in Munich; it is called Haile Selassie (Power of the Trinity). This is the new name which the emperor has assumed among his other titles; a heavy fine is threatened to anyone overheard referring to him as Tafari.

The words have become variously corrupted by the European visitors to 'Highly Salacious' and 'I love a lassie' – this last the inspiration of an RAC mechanic.

The bank and the manager's house are the two most solid buildings in the town; they stand behind a high wall in a side street between the two hotels. Round them are the two or three villas of the European traders, the bank officials, and the English chaplain. The shops are negligible; wretched tin stores, kept by Indians and Armenians, peddling tinned foods, lumps of coarse soap, and tarnished hardware. There is one shop of interest near the bank, kept by a French-speaking Abyssinian. It is called 'Curiosities' and exhibits anything from monkey-skins and cheap native jewellery to Amharic illuminated manuscripts of antiquity. Here I bought a number of modern Abyssinian paintings, mostly either hunting-scenes or intensely savage battle-pictures. Painting is more or less a hereditary craft in Abyssinia. It is in regular demand for ecclesiastical decoration. The churches of Abyssinia are all built on the same plan of a square inner sanctuary enclosed in two concentric ambulatories; sometimes the outside plan is octagonal, sometimes circular. It is very rarely that anyone except the priests is allowed to see into the sanctuary. Attention is concentrated on its walls, which are covered with frescos. The designs are traditional and are copied and recopied, generation after generation, with slight variation. When they begin to grow shabby and the church can afford it, a painter is called in to repaint them, as in Europe one calls in the paperhanger. In the intervals of executing these commissions the more skilful painters keep their hands in by doing secular work on sheets of linen or skins; these too are traditional in composition, but the artist is allowed more freedom in detail. His chief concern is to bring the old patterns up to date, and this he does, irrespective of historical propriety, by the introduction of topis, aeroplanes, and bombs. The secretary of the American Legation gave me a particularly delightful representation of the death of the Harar giant; this story is a very early mediæval legend, probably connected with the wars against the Arabs, but the artist has drawn the giant-slayers with the khaki uniforms and fixed bayonets of Tafari's latest guard – a happy change after the stale, half-facetious, pre-Raphaelite archaism that seems ineradicable in English taste.

The Gebbi is a great jumble of buildings on a hill to the east of the town. At night, during coronation week, it was lit up with rows of electric bulbs, but by day it presented a slightly dingy appearance. The nucleus consists of a stone building containing a throne-room and banqueting-hall; a glazed corridor runs down one side, many of the panes were broken and all were dirty; the front is furnished with a double staircase and portico, clearly of classic sympathies. It was made for Menelik by a French architect. (It might well have been the hôtel de ville of some French provincial town.) In

42

front of this is an untidy courtyard, irregular in shape, littered with loose stones and blown paper, and, all round it,
sheds and outbuildings of all kinds and sizes; tin guard-houses,
a pretty thatched chapel, barnlike apartments of various
Court officials, servants' quarters, laundry and kitchens, a
domed mausoleum in debased Byzantine style, a look-out
tower and a barrack square. High walls encircle the whole,
and the only approach, through which came alike butchers
and ambassadors, is through two heavily guarded doors. In
spite of this, the precincts seemed to be always full of loafers,
squatting and squabbling, or gaping at the visitors.

The American Legation is not far from the centre of the
town, but the British, French, and Italians all live beyond the
racecourse, five or six miles out. Menelik chose the site of
the concession, and the reason usually given for their remote-
ness is to ensure their safety in case of trouble. In point of
fact, they are wholly indefensible, and, if an attack were ever
made on them, would be unable to withstand half a day's
siege. The social result, for better or worse, has been to
divorce the diplomatic corps from the general life of the
town. It may be this that Menelik desired.

It is now possible to reach the British Legation by car;
until quite lately guests rode out to dinner on mules, a boy
running in front with a lantern. Indeed, as further preparation for the visitors, the road from the town had been
strewn with stones, and a motor-roller of the latest pattern

brought from Europe; this machine was sometimes seen heading for the legations, but some untoward event always interposed, and the greater part of the way was left to be rolled by the tyres of private cars. It was an expensive and bumpy journey.

The legation stands in a small park with the consulate next to it, and on either side of the drive a little garden city has sprung up of pretty thatched bungalows which accommodate the other officials. During the coronation a camp was pitched in the paddock for the staffs of the various visitors, and periodic bugling, reminiscent of an ocean liner, added a fresh incongruity to the bizarre life of the little community. At normal times this consisted of the Minister, lately arrived from Shanghai, a Chinese scholar whose life's work had been in the Far East; the secretary, lately arrived from Constantinople; the consul, lately arrived from Fez, an authority and enthusiast in Mohammedan law (none of these had yet had time to learn any Amharic); the archivist, who had spent five or six years at Addis and knew how to mark out tennis-courts; the vice-consul, who performed prodigies of skill in sorting out luggage and looking up trains, despite the fact that he was all the time seriously ill from the after-effects of blackwater fever, and the oriental secretary, whom a perfect command of Amharic and fair smattering of English made invaluable as official interpreter.

Besides the officials and officers of all grades who now

swelled the household, a substantial family party of uncles, aunts, and cousins had come out from England to see the fun. Housekeeping assumed a scale unprecedented in Addis Ababa, but all moved smoothly; a cook was specially imported from London who, happily enough, turned out to be named Mr Cook; the invitation cards from the British Legation greatly surpassed those of all other nations in thickness, area, and propriety of composition, and when it was discovered that by an engraver's error the name *Haile* had become *Hailu* (the name of the most formidable of the rival rases) no pains were spared to correct each card in pen and ink; the Duke's luggage was no sooner lost by one official than it was recovered by another. Everything bore witness to the triumph of Anglo-Saxon organisation.

Outside the legations was a personnel of supreme diversity. There was the Caucasian manager of the Haile Selassie Casino; the French editor of the *Courier d'Éthiope*, an infinitely helpful man, genial, punctilious, sceptical; an Englishman in the employ of the Abyssinian Government, debonair of appearance, but morbidly ill at ease in the presence of journalists before whom he might betray himself into some indiscretion; a French architect married to an Abyssinian; a bankrupt German planter obsessed by grievances; a tipsy old Australian prospector, winking over his whisky and hinting at the mountains full of platinum he could tell you about if he cared to. There was Mr Hall, in whose office I spent many frantic hours; he was a trader, of mixed German and Abyssinian descent, extremely handsome, well dressed, and monocled, a man of imperturbable courtesy, an exceptional linguist. During the coronation he had been put in a little tin house next to the Casino and constituted chief, and, as far as one could see, sole member, of a *bureau d'étrangers*. It was his week's task to listen to all the troubles of all the foreigners, official or unofficial, to distribute news to the Press, issue tickets and make out lists for the Abyssinian functions; if the Italian telegraph company took an hour's rest, it was Mr Hall who heard the complaints; if an officious police officer refused someone admittance to some grand stand, Mr Hall must see to it that the officer was reprimanded; if His Majesty's Stationery Office forgot to issue the text of the coronation service, Mr Hall promised everyone a copy; if a charabanc had not arrived to take the band to the racecourse, if there had not been enough coronation medals to go round the church, if, for any reason or no reason, anyone in Addis Ababa was in a bad temper – and at that altitude the most equable natures become unaccountably upset – off he went to Mr Hall. And whatever language he cared to speak, Mr Hall would understand and sympathise; with almost feminine delicacy he would calm him and compliment him; with masculine decision he would make a bold note of the affair on his pad; he would rise, bow, and smile his pacified visitor out with every graceful assurance of goodwill – and do absolutely nothing about it.

Of the Abyssinians we saw very little except as grave, rather stolid figures at the official receptions. There was Ras Hailu, owner of the rich province of Gojam, reputed wealthier than the emperor himself; a commanding figure, dark complexioned, and his little pointed beard dyed black, and slightly insolent eyes. Among his many great possessions was a night club two miles out on the Addis Alem road. He had planned this himself and, wishing to be up-to-date, had given it an English name. It was called 'Robinson'. There was the venerable Ras Kassa and Moulungetta, the commander-in-chief of the army, a mountain of a man with grey beard and bloodshot eyes; in full-dress uniform with scarlet-and-gold cloak and lion's mane busby, he looked hardly human; there was George Herui, son of the Minister of Foreign Affairs, the product of an English university – a slight young man dressed with great elegance either in European clothes or in the uniform of a Court page; his father stood high in the emperor's confidence; George's interest, however, seemed mainly Parisian.

Apart from the officials and journalists who pullulated at every corner, there were surprisingly few visitors. At one time Messrs Thomas Cook & Company were advertising a personally conducted tour, an announcement which took a great deal of the romance out of our expedition. The response was considerable, but when their agent arrived it soon became apparent that the enterprise was impracticable; there was no certainty of transport or accommodation, and, with soaring prices and fluctuating currency, it was impossible to give an estimate of the expenses involved. So the tour was cancelled, but the agent remained, a cocksure, dapper little Italian, an unfailing source of inaccurate information on all local topics.

There was a slightly class-conscious lady with a French title and an American accent, who left the town suddenly after a luncheon-party at which she was not accorded her proper precedence. There was the American professor, who will appear later in this narrative, and two formidable ladies in knitted suits and topis; though unrelated by blood, long companionship had made them almost indistinguishable, square-jawed, tight-lipped, with hard, discontented eyes. For them the whole coronation was a profound disappointment. What did it matter that they were witnesses of a unique stage of the interpenetration of two cultures? They were out for Vice. They were collecting material, in fact, for a little book on the subject, an African *Mother India*, and every minute devoted to Coptic ritual or displays of horsemanship was a minute wasted. Prostitution and drug traffic comprised their modest interests, and they were too dense to find evidence of either.

But perhaps the most remarkable visitors were the Marine band. At first the emperor had intended to import a European dance-band from Cairo, but the estimate for fees and expenses was so discouraging that he decided instead to issue an invitation to the band of HMS *Effingham* to attend the coronation as his guests and to play at the various functions. They arrived on the same day as the Duke of Gloucester, under the command of Major Sinclair, strengthened by a diet of champagne at breakfast, luncheon, tea, and dinner throughout their journey, and much sage advice about the propriety of their behaviour in a foreign capital. At Addis they were quartered in a large, unfinished hotel; each man had his own bedroom, furnished by his thoughtful hosts with hairbrushes, clothes-hangers, and brand-new enamelled spittoons.

Perhaps no one did more to deserve his star of Ethiopia than Major Sinclair. Eschewing the glitter and dignity of the legation camp, he loyally remained with his men in the town, and spent anxious days arranging appointments that were never kept; his diary, which some of us were privileged to see, was a stark chronicle of successive disappointments patiently endured. '*Appointment 9.30 emperor's private secretary to arrange for this evening's banquet; he did not come. 11. Went as arranged to see master of the king's music; he was not there. 12. Went to see Mr Hall to obtain score of Ethiopian national anthem — not procurable. 2.30. Car should have come to take men to aerodrome — did not arrive . . .*' and so on. But, in spite of every discouragement, the band was always present on time, irreproachably dressed, and provided with the correct music.

One morning in particular, on which the band played a conspicuous part, remains vividly in my memory as typical of the whole week. It was the first day of the official celebrations, to be inaugurated by the unveiling of the new Menelik memorial. The ceremony was announced for ten o'clock. Half an hour before the time, Irene Ravensdale and I drove to the spot. Here, on the site of the old execution-tree, stood the monument, shrouded in brilliant green silk. Round it was a little ornamental garden with paving, a balustrade, and regular plots, from which, here and there, emerged delicate shoots of newly sown grass. While some workmen were laying carpets on the terrace and spreading yellow sunshades of the kind which cover the tables at open-air restaurants, others were still chipping at the surrounding masonry and planting drooping palm-trees in the arid beds. A heap of gilt arm-chairs lay on one side; on the other a mob of photographers and movietone men were fighting for places. Opposite the carpeted terrace rose a stand of several unstable tiers. A detachment of policemen were engaged furiously laying about them with canes in the attempt to keep these seats clear of natives. Four or five Europeans were already established there. Irene and I joined them. Every ten minutes or so a police officer would appear and order us all off; we produced our *laissez-passers*; he saluted and went away, to be succeeded at a short interval by a colleague, when the performance was repeated.

The square and half a mile of the avenue approaching it were lined with royal guards; there was a band formed up in front of them; the Belgian colonel curvetted about on an uneasy chestnut horse. Presently, punctual to the minute, appeared Major Sinclair and his band. They had had to march from their hotel, as the charabanc ordered for them had failed to appear. They halted, and Major Sinclair approached the Belgian colonel for instructions. The colonel knew no English, and the major no French; an embarrassing interview followed, complicated by the caprices of the horse, which plunged backwards and sideways over the square. In this way the two officers covered a large area of ground, conversing inconclusively the while with extravagant gestures. Eventually Irene heroically stepped out to interpret for them. It appeared that the Belgian colonel had had no orders about the English band. He had his own band there and did not want another. The major explained he had direct instructions to appear in the square at ten. The colonel said the major could not possibly stay in the square; there was no room for him, and anyway he would have no opportunity of playing, since the native band had a programme of music fully adequate for the whole proceedings. (Knowing that band's tendency to repetition, we could well believe it.) At last the colonel conceded that the English band might take up a position at the extreme end of his troops at the bottom of the hill. The officers parted, and the band marched away out of sight. A long wait followed, while the battle between police and populace raged round the stand. At last the delegations began to arrive; the soldiers presented arms; the native band played the appropriate music; the Belgian colonel was borne momentarily backwards through the ranks, capered heroically among the crowd, and reappeared at another corner of the square. The delegations took up their places on the gilt chairs under the umbrellas. A long pause preceded the emperor's arrival; the soldiers still stood stiff. Suddenly up that imposing avenue there appeared a slave, trotting unconcernedly with a gilt chair on his head. He put it among the others, looked round with interest at the glittering uniforms, and then retired. At last the emperor came; first a troop of lancers, then the crimson car and silk umbrella. He took up his place in the centre of the Court under a blue canopy; the band played the Ethiopian national anthem. A secretary presented him with the text of his speech; the cameramen began snapping and turning. But there was a fresh delay. Something had gone wrong. Messages passed from mouth to mouth; a runner disappeared down the hill.

One photographer, bolder than the rest, advanced out of the crowd and planted his camera within a few yards of the royal party; he wore a violet suit of plus-fours, a green shirt open at the neck, tartan stockings, and parti-coloured shoes. After a few happy shots of the emperor he walked slowly along the line, looking the party critically up and down.

When he found anyone who attracted his attention, he took a photograph of him. Then, expressing his satisfaction with a slight inclination of the head, he rejoined his colleagues.

Still a delay. Then up the avenue came Major Sinclair and the Marine band. They halted in the middle of the square, arranged their music, and played the national anthem. Things were then allowed to proceed according to plan. The emperor advanced, read his speech, and pulled the cord. There was a rending of silk and a vast equestrian figure in gilt bronze was partially revealed. Men appeared with poles and poked away the clinging folds. One piece, out of reach of their efforts, obstinately fluttered over the horse's ears and eyes. The Greek contractor mounted a ladder and dislodged the rag.

The Marine band continued to play; the delegations and courtiers made for their cars; the emperor paused, and listened attentively to the music, then smiled his approval to the major before driving away. As the last of the visitors disappeared, the people broke through the soldiers, and the square became a dazzle of white tunics and black heads. For many days to come, numbers of them might be seen clustering round the memorial and gazing with puzzled awe at this new ornament to their city.

Three

Until late on the preceding afternoon, wild uncertainty prevailed about the allocation of tickets for the coronation. The
legations knew nothing. Mr Hall knew nothing, and his
office was continuously besieged by anxious journalists
whose only hope of getting their reports back in time for
Monday's papers was to write and dispatch them well before
the event. What could they say when they did not even know
where the ceremony would take place?

With little disguised irritation they set to work making
the best of their meagre material. Gorgis and its precincts
were impenetrably closed; a huge tent could be discerned
through the railings, built against one wall of the church.
Some described the actual coronation as taking place there;
others used it as the scene of a state reception and drew
fanciful pictures of the ceremony in the interior of the cathedral, 'murky, almost suffocating with incense and the thick, stifling smoke
of tallow candles' (Associated Press); authorities on Coptic ritual remarked that as the coronation proper must take place
in the inner sanctuary, which no layman might glimpse,
much less enter, there was small hope of anyone seeing any-

thing at all, unless, conceivably, exceptions were made of the Duke of Gloucester and Prince Udine. The cinema-men, whose companies had spent very large sums in importing them and their talking apparatus, began to show signs of restlessness, and some correspondents became almost menacing in their representations of the fury of a slighted Press. Mr Hall, however, remained his own serene self. Everything, he assured us, was being arranged for our particular convenience; only, he admitted, the exact details were still unsettled.

Eventually, about fourteen hours before the ceremony was due to start, numbered tickets were issued through the legations; there was plenty of room for all, except, as it happened, for the Abyssinians themselves. The rases and Court officials were provided with gilt chairs, but the local chiefs seemed to be wholly neglected; most of them remained outside, gazing wistfully at the ex-Kaiser's coach and the tall hats of the European and American visitors; those that succeeded in pushing their way inside were kept far at the back, where they squatted together on their haunches, or, in all the magnificent trappings of their gala dress, dozed simply in distant corners of the great tent.

For it was there, in the end, that the service took place. 'Tent', however, gives an incomplete impression of this fine pavilion. It was light and lofty, supported by two colonnades of draped scaffold-poles; the east end was hung with silk curtains, behind which a sanctuary had been improvised to hold the tabot from the cathedral. A carpeted dais ran half the length of the floor. On it stood the silk-covered table that bore the regalia and the crown neatly concealed in a cardboard hat-box; on either side were double rows of gilt chairs for the Court and the diplomatic corps, and at the end, with their backs to the body of the hall, two canopied thrones, one scarlet for the emperor and one blue for the empress.

Their Majesties had spent the night in vigil, surrounded inside the cathedral by clergy, and outside by troops; when they entered the tent it was from behind the curtains by means of a side door leading directly from the cathedral. One enterprising journalist headed his report 'Meditation Behind Machine-Guns', and had the gratifying experience when he was at last admitted into the precincts, of finding his guess fully justified; a machine section was posted on the steps covering each approach. Other predictions were less happy. Many correspondents, for instance, wrote accounts of the emperor's solemn progress from the palace at sundown; actually it was late at night before he arrived, and then with the minimum of display. The Associated Press postponed the event until dawn, and described it in these terms: 'As their Majesties rode to church through the dusty streets of the mountain capital, which were packed with tens of thousands of their braves and chieftains, the masses uttered savage cries of acclaim. Scores of natives were trampled in the dust as the crowd surged to catch sight of the coronation party.'

It was highly interesting to me, when the papers began to arrive from Europe and America, to compare my own experiences with those of the different correspondents. I had the fortune to be working for a paper which values the accuracy of its news before everything else; even so I was betrayed into a few mistakes. Telegraphic economy accounts for some of these, as when 'Abuna', the title of the Abyssinian primate, became expanded by a zealous subeditor into 'the Archbishop of Abuna'. Proper names often came through somewhat mangled, and curious transpositions of whole phrases occasionally took place, so that somewhere between Addis Ababa and London I was saddled with the amazing assertion that George Herui had served on Sir John Maffey's staff in the Soudan. Some mistakes of this kind seem inevitable. My surprise in reading the Press reports of the coronation was not that my more impetuous colleagues had allowed themselves to be slapdash about their details or that they had fallen into some occasional exaggeration of the more romantic and incongruous aspects of the affair. It seemed to me that we had been witnesses of a quite different series of events. 'Getting in first with the news' and 'giving the public what it wants', the two dominating principles of Fleet Street, are not always reconcilable.

I do not intend by this any conventional condemnation of the 'Yellow Press'. It seems to me that a prig is someone who judges people by his own, rather than by their, standards;

criticism only becomes useful when it can show people where their own principles are in conflict. It is perfectly natural that the cheaper newspapers should aim at entertainment rather than instruction, and give prominence to what is startling and frivolous over what is important but unamusing or unintelligible. 'If a dog bites a man, that's nothing; if a man bites a dog, that's news.' My complaint is that in its scramble for precedence the cheap Press is falling short of the very standards of public service it has set itself. Almost any London newspaper, today, would prefer an incomplete, inaccurate, and insignificant report of an event provided it came in time for an earlier edition than its rivals. Now the public is not concerned with this competition. The reader, opening his paper on the breakfast-table, has no vital interest in, for instance, Abyssinian affairs. An aeroplane accident or boxing-match are a different matter. In these cases he simply wants to know the result as soon as possible. But the coronation of an African emperor means little or nothing to him. He may read about it on Monday or Tuesday, he will not be impatient. All he wants from Africa is something to amuse him in the railway train to his office. He will be just as much amused on Tuesday as on Monday. The extra day's delay makes the difference, to the correspondent on the spot, of whether he has time to compose a fully informed account (and, in almost all cases, the better informed the account the more entertaining it will be to the reader). Or at least it makes this difference. Events in a newspaper become amusing and thrilling just in so far as they are given credence as historical facts. Anyone, sitting down for a few hours with a typewriter, could compose a paper that would be the ideal of every news-editor. He would deal out dramatic deaths in the royal family, derail trains, embroil the country in civil war, and devise savage and insoluble murders. All these things would be profoundly exciting to the reader so long as he thought they were true. If they were offered to him as fiction they would be utterly insignificant. (And this shows the great gulf which divides the novelist from the journalist. The value of a novel depends on the standards each book evolves for itself; incidents which have no value as news are given any degree of importance according to their place in the book's structure and their relation to other incidents in the composition, just as subdued colours attain great intensity in certain pictures.) The delight of reading the popular newspapers does not come, except quite indirectly, from their political programmes or 'feature articles', but from the fitful illumination which glows in odd places – phrases reported from the police courts, statements made in public orations in provincial towns – which suddenly reveal unexpected byways of life. If these were pure invention they would lose all interest. As soon as one knows that they are written with conscious satire by some bright young reporter in the office, there is no further amusement in the astounding opinions so dogmatically expressed in the correspondence column.

In Addis Ababa, for the first time, I was able to watch the machinery of journalism working in a simplified form. A London office is too full and complicated to enable one to form opinions on any brief acquaintance. Here I knew most of the facts and people involved, and in the light of this knowledge I found the Press reports shocking and depressing. After all, there really was something there to report that was quite new to the European public; a succession of events of startling spectacular character, and a system of life, in a tangle of modernism and barbarity, European, African, and American, of definite, individual character. It seemed to me that here, at least, the truth was stranger than the newspaper reports. For instance, one newspaper stated that the emperor's banqueting-hall was decorated with inlaid marble, ivory, and malachite. That is not very strange to anyone who has been into any of the cheaper London hotels. In actual fact there were photographs of Mr Ramsay MacDonald and M. Poincaré, and a large, very lifelike oil-painting of a lion, by an Australian artist. It all depends on what one finds amusing. In the same way the royal coach was reported to have been drawn from the church by six milk-white horses – a wholly banal conception of splendour. If the reporters had wanted to say something thrilling, why did they not say gilded eunuchs, or ostriches with dyed plumes, or a team of captive kings, blinded and wearing yokes of elephant tusk? But since custom or poverty of imagination confined them to the stables, why should they not content themselves with what actually happened, that the ex-Kaiser's coach appeared at the church equipped with six horses (they were not white, but that is immaterial) and a Hungarian coachman in fantastic circus livery, but that, as they had never been properly trained, they proved difficult to manage and at the first salute of guns fell into utter confusion, threatening destruction to the coach and causing grave alarm to the surrounding crowds; that finally two had to be unharnessed, and that this was not accomplished until one groom had been seriously injured; that next day in the procession the coachman did not appear, and the emperor resumed his crimson motor car – a triumph of modernism typical of the whole situation?

This is what I saw at the coronation:

The emperor and empress were due to appear from their vigil at seven in the morning. We were warned to arrive at the tent about an hour before that time. Accordingly, having dressed by candlelight, Irene and I proceeded there at about six. For many hours before dawn the roads into the town had been filled with tribesmen coming in from the surrounding camps. We could see them passing the hotel (the street lamps were working that night) in dense white crowds, some riding mules, some walking, some moving at a slow trot beside their masters. All, as always, were armed. Our car moved slowly to Gorgis, hooting continuously. There were many other cars; some carrying Europeans; others, Abyssinian officials. Eventually we reached the church and were admitted after a narrow scrutiny of our tickets and ourselves. The square inside the gates was comparatively clear; from the top of the steps the machine-guns compromised with ecclesiastical calm. From inside the cathedral came the voices of the priests singing the last phase of the service that had lasted all night. Eluding the numerous soldiers, police-men, and officials who directed us towards the tent, we slipped into the outer ambulatory of the church, where the choir of bearded and vested deacons were dancing to the music of hand drums and little silver rattles. The drummers squatted round them; but they carried the rattles themselves and in their other hand waved praying-sticks.[1] Some carried nothing, but merely clapped their empty palms. They shuf-fled in and out, singing and swaying; the dance was performed with body and arms rather than with the feet. Their faces expressed the keenest enjoyment – almost, in some cases, ecstasy. The brilliant morning sun streamed in on them from the windows, on their silver crosses, silver-headed rods, and on the large, illuminated manuscript from

1. These are long rods with crooked handles; the Abyssinians prostrate themselves frequently, but do not kneel in prayer; instead, they stand resting their hands on the stick and their forehead on their hands.

which one of them, undeterred by the music, was reciting the Gospels; the clouds of incense mounted and bellied in the shafts of light.

Presently we went on to the tent. This was already well filled. The clothes of the congregation varied considerably. Most of the men were wearing morning coats, but some had appeared in evening dress and one or two in dinner-jackets. One lady had stuck an American flag in the top of her sun-helmet. The junior members of the legations were there already, in uniform, fussing among the seats to see that everything was in order. By seven o'clock the delegations arrived. The English party, led by the Duke of Gloucester and Lord Airlie in hussar and lancer uniforms, were undoubtedly the most august, though there was a very smart Swede carrying a silver helmet. It happened that our delegation was largely composed of men of unusually imposing physique; it was gratifying both to our own national loyalty (an emotion which becomes surprisingly sensible in remote places) and also to that of the simpler Abyssinians, who supposed, rightly enough, that this magnificent array was there with the unequivocal purpose of courtesy towards the emperor; I am rather more doubtful, however, about the impression made on the less uneducated classes. They have deep suspicions of the intentions of their European neighbours, and the parade of our own war lords (as Sir John Maffey, Sir Harold Kittermaster, Sir Stewart Symes, Admiral Fullerton, and Mr Noble, in full uniform, may well have appeared in their eyes) was little calculated to allay them. It is perhaps significant to note that important commercial contracts and advisory positions at Court have recently been accorded to the least demonstrative of the visiting nations – the United States of America. However, it is churlish to complain that our public servants are too handsome, and, as far as the coronation ceremonies went, they certainly added glamour to the pageant.

It was long after the last delegate had taken his place that the emperor and empress appeared from the church. We could hear the singing going on behind the curtains. Photographers, amateur and professional, employed the time in taking furtive snapshots. Reporters dispatched their boys to the telegraph office with supplementary accounts of the preliminaries. By some misunderstanding of the instructions of the responsible official, the office was closed for the day. After the manner of native servants, the messengers, instead of reporting the matter to their masters, sat, grateful for the rest, on the steps gossiping until it should open. It was late in the day that the truth became known, and then there was more trouble for Mr Hall.

The ceremony was immensely long, even according to the original schedule, and the clergy succeeded in prolonging it by at least an hour and a half beyond the allotted time. The six succeeding days of celebration were to be predominantly military, but the coronation day itself was in the hands of the Church, and they were going to make the most of it. Psalms, canticles, and prayers succeeded each other, long passages of Scripture were read, all in the extinct ecclesiastical tongue, Ghiz. Candles were lit one by one; the coronation oaths were proposed and sworn; the diplomats shifted uncomfortably in their gilt chairs, noisy squabbles broke out round the entrance between the imperial guard and the retainers of the local chiefs. Professor W., who was an expert of high transatlantic reputation on Coptic ritual, occasionally re-marked: 'They are beginning the Mass now', 'That was the offertory', 'No, I was wrong; it was the consecration', 'No, I was wrong; I think it is the secret Gospel', 'No, I think it must be the Epistle', 'How very curious; I don't believe it was a Mass at all', 'Now they *are* beginning the Mass . . .' and so on. Presently the bishops began to fumble among the band-boxes, and investiture began. At long intervals the emperor was presented with robe, orb, spurs, spear, and finally with the crown. A salute of guns was fired, and the crowds out-side, scattered all over the surrounding waste spaces, began to cheer; the imperial horses reared up, plunged on top of each other, kicked the gilding off the front of the coach, and broke their traces. The coachman sprang from the box and whipped them from a safe distance. Inside the pavilion there was a general sense of relief; it had all been very fine and impressive, now for a cigarette, a drink, and a change into less formal costume. Not a bit of it. The next thing was to crown the empress and the heir apparent; another salvo of guns followed, during which an Abyssinian groom had two ribs broken in an attempt to unharness a pair of the imperial horses. Again we felt for our hats and gloves. But the Coptic choir still sang; the bishops then proceeded to take back the regalia with proper prayers, lections, and canticles.

'I have noticed some very curious variations in the canon of the Mass,' remarked the professor, 'particularly with regard to the kiss of peace.'

Then the Mass began.

For the first time throughout the morning the emperor and empress left their thrones; they disappeared behind the curtains into the improvised sanctuary; most of the clergy went too. The stage was empty save for the diplomats; their faces were set and strained, their attitudes inelegant. I have seen just that look in crowded second-class railway carriages, at dawn, between Avignon and Marseille. Their clothes made them funnier still. Marshal d'Esperez alone preserved his dignity, his chest thrown out, his baton poised on his knee, rigid as a war memorial, and, as far as one could judge, wide awake.

It was now about eleven o'clock, the time at which the emperor was due to leave the pavilion. Punctually to plan, three Abyssinian aeroplanes rose to greet him. They circled round and round over the tent, eagerly demonstrating their newly acquired art of swooping and curvetting within a few feet of the canvas roof. The noise was appalling; the local chiefs stirred in their sleep and rolled on to their faces; only by the opening and closing of their lips and the turning of their music could we discern that the Coptic deacons were still singing.

'A most unfortunate interruption. I missed many of the verses,' said the professor.

Eventually, at about half-past twelve, the Mass came to an end and the emperor and empress, crowned, shuffling along under a red and gold canopy, and looking as Irene remarked, exactly like the processional statues of Seville, crossed to a grand stand, from which the emperor delivered a royal proc-lamation; an aeroplane scattered copies of the text and, through loud-speakers, the Court heralds reread it to the populace.

There was a slightly ill-tempered scramble among the photographers and cinema-men – I received a heavy blow in the middle of the back from a large camera, and a hoarse rebuke, 'Come along there now – let the eyes of the world see.'

Dancing broke out once more among the clergy, and there is no knowing how long things might not have gone on, had not the photographers so embarrassed and jostled them, and outraged their sense of reverence, that they withdrew to fin-ish their devotions alone in the cathedral.

Then at last the emperor and empress were conducted to

their coach and borne off to luncheon by its depleted but still demonstratively neurasthenic team of horses.

Having finished the report for my paper, which I had been composing during the service, I delivered it to the wireless operator at the Italian Legation; as I began to search for my car the Belgian major rose up and began insulting me; I could not quite understand why until I learned that he mistook me for a German bank-clerk who apparently had lately boxed the ears of his orderly. My Indian chauffeur had got bored and gone home. Luncheon at the hotel was odious. All food supplies had been commandeered by the Government, M. Hallot told us; it was rather doubtful whether the market would open again until the end of the week. Meanwhile there were tinned chunks of pineapple and three courses of salt beef, one cut in small cubes with chopped onion, one left in a slab with tomato ketchup, one in slices with hot water and Worcestershire sauce; the waiters had gone out the night before to get drunk and had not yet woken up.

We were all in a bad temper that night.

Six days followed of intensive celebration. On Monday morning the delegations were required to leave wreaths at the mausoleum of Menelik and Zauditu. This is a circular, domed building of vaguely Byzantine affinities, standing in the Gebbi grounds. Its interior is furnished with oil-paintings and enlarged photographs of the royal family, a fumed oak grandfather clock, and a few occasional tables of the kind exhibited in shop windows in Tottenham Court Road; their splay legs protruded from under embroidered linen table-cloths, laid diagonally; on them stood little conical silver vases of catkins boldly counterfeited in wire and magenta wool. Steps led down to the vault where lay the white marble sarcophagi of the two potentates. It is uncertain whether either contains the body attributed to it, or indeed any body at all. The date and place of Menelik's death are a palace secret, but it is generally supposed to have taken place about two years before its formal announcement to people; the empress probably lies out under the hill at Debra Lebanos. At various hours that morning, however, the delegations of the Great Powers dutifully appeared with fine bundles of flowers, and, not to be outdone in reverence, Professor W. came tripping gravely in with a little bunch of white carnations.

There was a cheerful, friendly tea-party that afternoon at the American Legation and a ball and firework display at the Italian, but the party which excited the keenest interest was the *gebbur* given by the emperor to his tribesmen. These banquets are a regular feature of Ethiopian life, constituting, in fact, a vital bond between the people and their overlords, whose prestige in time of peace varied directly with their frequency and abundance. Until a few years ago attendance at a *gebbur* was part of the entertainment offered to every visitor in Abyssinia. Copious first-hand accounts can be found in almost every book about the country, describing the packed, squatting ranks of the diners; the slaves carrying the warm quarters of newly slaughtered, uncooked beef; the dispatch with which each guest carves for himself; the upward slice of his dagger with which he severs each mouthful from the dripping lump; the flat, damp platters of local bread; the great draughts of *tedj* and *talla* from the horn drinking-pots; the butchers outside felling and dividing the oxen; the emperor and nobles at the high table, exchanging highly seasoned morsels of more elaborate fare. These are the traditional features of the *gebbur* and, no doubt, of this occasion also. It was thus that the journalists described their impressions in glowing paraphrases of Rhey and Kingsford. When the time came, however, we found that particular precautions had been taken to exclude all Europeans from the spectacle. Perhaps it was felt that the feast might give a false impression of the civilising pretensions of the Government. Mr Hall loyally undertook to exercise his influence for each of us personally, but in the end no one gained admission except two resolute ladies and, by what was felt to be a very base exploitation of racial advantage, the coloured correspondent of a syndicate of negro newspapers.

All that I saw was the last relay of guests shambling out of the Gebbi gates late that afternoon. They were a very enviable company, quite stupefied with food and drink. Policemen attempted to herd them on, kicking their insensible backs and whacking them with canes, but nothing disturbed their serene good temper. The chiefs were hoisted on to mules by their retainers and remained there blinking and smiling; one very old man, mounted back to front, felt feebly about the crupper for his reins; some stood clasped together in silent, swaying groups; others, lacking support, rolled contentedly in the dust. I remembered them that evening as I sat in the supper-room at the Italian Legation gravely discussing the slight disturbance of diplomatic propriety caused by the emperor's capricious distribution of honours.

There were several parties that week, of more or less identical composition. At three there were fireworks, resulting in at least one nasty accident; at one, a cinema which failed to work; at one, Gilla dancers who seemed to dislocate their shoulders, and sweated so heartily that our host was able to plaster their foreheads with bank-notes; at another, Somali dancers shivered with cold on a lawn illuminated with coloured flares. There was a race meeting, where the local ponies plunged over low jumps and native jockeys cut off corners; the emperor sat all alone under a great canopy; the royal enclosure was packed and the rest of the course empty of spectators; a totalisator paid out four dollars on every winning three-dollar ticket; both bands played; Prince Udine presented an enormous cup and the emperor a magnificent kind of urn whose purpose no one could discover; it had several silver taps and little silver stands, and a great tray covered with silver cups of the kind from which grape-fruit is eaten in cinema-films. This fine trophy was won by a gentleman, in gilt riding-boots, attached to the French Legation, and was used later at their party for champagne. There was a certain amount of whispering against French sportsmanship, however, as they had sent back their books of sweepstake tickets with scarcely one sold. This showed a very bad club spirit, the other legations maintained.

There was a procession of all the troops, uniformed and irregular, in the middle of which Irene appeared in a taxi-cab surprisingly surrounded by a band of mounted musicians playing six-foot pipes and banging on saddle drums of oxhide and wood. The people all shrilled their applause, as the emperor passed, in a high, wailing whistle.

There was the opening of a museum of souvenirs, containing examples of native craftsmanship, the crown captured by General Napier at Magdala and returned by the Victoria and Albert Museum, and a huge, hollow stone which an Abyssinian saint had worn as a hat.

There was a review of the troops on the plain outside the railway station. Although we had been privileged to see almost every member of His Majesty's forces almost every day, this was a startling display for those, like myself, who had never seen a muster of tribesmen in Arabia or Morocco. The men converged on the royal stand from all over the plain, saluting him with cries and flourishes of arms, the little horses and mules galloping right up to the foot of the throne and being reined back savagely on to their haunches, with mouths dripping foam and blood.

But no catalogue of events can convey any real idea of these astounding days, of an atmosphere utterly unique, elusive, unforgettable. If in the foregoing pages I have seemed to give undue emphasis to the irregularity of the proceedings, to their unpunctuality, and their occasional failure, it is because this was an essential part of their character and charm. In Addis Ababa everything was haphazard and incongruous; one learned always to expect the unusual and yet was always surprised.

Every morning we awoke to a day of brilliant summer sunshine; every evening fell cool, limpid, charged with hidden vitality, fragrant with the thin smoke of the *tukal* fires, pulsing, like a live body, with the beat of the tom-toms that drummed incessantly somewhere out of sight among the eucalyptus-trees. In this rich African setting were jumbled together, for a few days, people of every race and temper, all involved in one way or another in that complex of hysteria and apathy, majesty and farce; a company shot through with every degree of animosity and suspicion. There were continual rumours born of the general uncertainty; rumours about the date and place of every ceremony; rumours of dissension in high places; rumours that, in the absence at Addis Ababa of all the responsible officials, the interior was seething with brigandage; rumours that Sir Percival Phillips had used the legation wireless; that the Ethiopian Minister to Paris had been refused admittance to Addis Ababa; that the royal coachman had not had his wages for two months and had given in his notice; that the airmen from Aden were secretly prospecting for a service between the capital and the coast; that one of the legations had refused to receive the empress's first lady-in-waiting; above all, there was the great Flea Scandal and the Indiscretion about the Duke of Glouces-ter's Cook.

I had an intimation of that affair some days before it was generally known. Two journalists were drinking cocktails with me on the hotel terrace on the evening before the cor-onation. One of them said, 'We got a jolly good story this morning out of —,' naming an amiable nitwit on the Duke of Gloucester's staff. 'It isn't in your paper's line, so I don't mind telling you.'

The story was plain and credible; first, that the old Gebbi in which His Royal Highness was quartered was, like most houses in Ethiopia, infested with fleas; secondly, that the German cook was unable to obtain due attention from the native servants and came to complain of the fact. She paced up and down the room passionately, explaining her difficul-ties; when she turned her back it was apparent that in her agitation she had failed to fasten her skirt, which fell open and revealed underclothes of red flannel; the English party

were unable to hide their amusement, and the cook, thinking that the ridicule was part of a scheme of persecution,
stormed out of the house, leaving the party without their
breakfast.

'You sent that back?' I asked.

'You bet your life I did.'

I felt there might be trouble.

Two days later the local correspondent of one of the
news agencies received the following message from London:
'*Investigate report fleas Gloucester's bed also cook red drawers left Duke
breakfastless.*' He hurried with this cable to the legation and,
on the Minister's advice cabled back, '*Insignificant incident greatly
exaggerated advisable suppress.*'

But it was too late. The papers of the civilised world had
published the story. The emperor's European agents had
cabled back news of the betrayal; the emperor had com-
plained to the legations. Stirring reports were in circulation
that the emperor required every journalist to leave the country, bag and baggage, within twenty-four hours; that Lady
Barton was revising her dance list; that the kantaba had cancelled his banquet; that no more stars of Ethiopia were to be
dealt out until the culprit was discovered. Phrases such as
'breach of hospitality', 'gross ill-breeding', 'unpardonable
irregularity', 'damned bad form' volleyed and echoed on
every side. At a party that evening the ADC who had caused
the trouble was conspicuously vigorous in his aspirations to

'kick the bounder's backside, whoever he is'. We all felt uneasy for nearly a day, until the topic was succeeded by the French Legation's shabby behaviour over the sweepstake tickets, and the grave question of whether the emperor would attend Marshal d'Esperez's private tea-party.

One morning, a few days later, Irene and I were sitting outside the hotel drinking apéritifs and waiting for luncheon; we were entertained by the way in which the various visitors treated a pedlar who diffidently approached them with a bundle of bootlaces in one hand and an enamelled *pot de chambre* in the other. Suddenly a taxi drove up, and a servant wearing the palace livery jumped out and emptied a large pile of envelopes into Irene's lap. Two were addressed to us. We took them and handed back the rest, which the man presented, to be sorted in the same way, at the next table. It was not perhaps the most expeditious method of delivery, but, as he was unable to read, it is difficult to think of what else he could have done.

The envelopes contained an invitation to lunch with the emperor that day at one o'clock; as it was then after half-past twelve we disregarded the request for an answer and hurried off to change.

Professor W. had spoken to me of this party some days before, saying with restrained relish, 'On Saturday I am lunching with the emperor. There are several things I shall be interested to discuss with him.' But, as it turned out, he had little opportunity for conversation. There were about eighty guests and many empty places, showing that the messenger had not been able to finish his round in time (indeed, it is no unusual thing in Addis Ababa to receive cards of invitation many hours after the event). They were the European officials in the Abyssinian Government, European residents, journalists, and private visitors whose names had been sent in by the legations; the European officers of the army, a few Abyssinian notables, the wives of visiting consuls, and so on. At first we stood in the glazed corridor which ran down one side of the main building. Then we were ushered into the throne-room, bowed and curtseyed, and ranged ourselves round the walls while *byrrh* and vermouth and cigars were carried round. There was something slightly ecclesiastical in the atmosphere.

The emperor then led the way into the dining-room. We tramped in behind him in no particular order. He seated himself at the centre of the top table; three tables ran at right angles to him, resplendent with gold plate and white-and-gold china. Typewritten name-cards lay on each plate. Ten minutes or so followed of some confusion as we jostled round and round looking for our places; there was no plan of the table, and as most of us were complete strangers we were unable to help each other. The emperor sat watching us with a placid little smile. We must have looked very amusing. Naturally no one cared to look at the places next to the emperor, so that when at last we were all seated the two most honoured guests were left to sidle forlornly into the nearest empty places. Eventually they were fetched. Irene sat on one side and the French wife of the Egyptian consul on his other. I sat between an English airman and a Belgian photographer. A long meal followed, of many courses of fair French cooking and good European wines. There was also *tedj* and the national beverage made from fermented honey. We had sent out for some, one evening at the hotel, and found it an opaque yellowish liquid, mild and rather characterless. The emperor's *tedj* was a very different drink, quite clear, slightly brown, heavy, rich, and dry. After luncheon, at Irene's request, we were given some of the liqueur distilled from it – a colourless spirit of fine flavour and disconcerting potency.

Only one odd thing happened at luncheon. Just as we were finishing, a stout young woman rose from a seat near the back and made her way resolutely between the tables until she planted herself within a few yards of the emperor. I understand that she was a Syrian Jewess employed in some educational capacity in the town. She carried a sheaf of papers which she held close to her pince-nez with one plump hand while she raised the other above her head in a Fascist salute. Conversation faltered and ceased. The emperor looked at her with kindly inquiry. Then, in a voice of peculiar strength and stridency, she began to recite an ode. It was a very long complimentary ode, composed by herself in Arabic, a language wholly unintelligible to His Majesty. Between verses she made a long pause during which she fluttered her manuscript; then she began again. We had just begun to feel that the performance would really prove interminable, when, just as suddenly as she had begun, she stopped, bobbed, turned about, and, with glistening forehead and slightly labouring breath, strode back to her place to receive the congratulations of her immediate neighbours. The emperor rose and led the way back to the throne-room. Here we stood round the walls for a quarter of an hour while liqueurs were served. Then we bowed in turn and filed out into the sunshine.

That evening at the hotel two soldiers appeared with a huge basket of coloured Harari work for Irene from the emperor. In it was a fine outfit of native woman's clothing, consisting of a pair of black satin trousers of great girth, an embroidered cloak, a hand-woven *chamma*, and a set of gold ornaments.

One moment of that week is particularly vivid in my memory. It was late at night and we had just returned from a party. My room, as I have said, was in an outhouse at a little distance from the hotel; a grey horse, some goats, and the hotel guard, his head wrapped in a blanket, were sleeping in the yard as I went across. Behind my room, separated from the hotel grounds by wooden palings, lay a cluster of native *tukals*. That evening there was a party in one of them – probably celebrating a wedding or funeral. The door faced my way and

I could see a glimmer of lamplight in the interior. They were singing a monotonous song, clapping in time and drumming with their hands on petrol-tins. I suppose there were about ten or fifteen of them there. I stood for some time listening. I was wearing a tall hat, evening clothes and white gloves. Presently the guard woke up and blew a little trumpet; the sound was taken up by other guards at neighbouring houses (it is in this way that they assure their employers of their vigilance); then he wrapped himself once more in his blanket and relapsed into sleep.

The song continued unvarying in the still night. The absurdity of the whole week became suddenly typified for me in that situation – my preposterous clothes, the sleeping animals, and the wakeful party on the other side of the stockade.

Four

It was during our third week in Addis Ababa, when the official celebrations were over and the delegations were being packed off to the coast as fast as the Franco-Ethiopian Railway's supply of sleeping-cars would allow, that Professor W. suggested to me that we should make an expedition together to Debra Lebanos.

This monastery has for four centuries been the centre of Abyssinian spiritual life. It is built round a spring where the waters of Jordan, conveyed subterraneously down the Red Sea, are believed to well up endowed with curative properties; pilgrims go there from all parts of the country, and it is a popular burial-ground for those who can afford it, since all found there at the Last Trump are assured of unimpeded entry into Paradise.

It was the dry season, so that the road could be attempted by car. Professor Mercer had recently made the journey and had come back with photographs of a hitherto unknown version of Ecclesiastes. Ras Kassa had driven from Fiche only two weeks before and renewed the bridges for the occasion, so that we had little difficulty in finding a driver willing to take us. Permission had first to be obtained from Kassa to use the road. Professor W. obtained this and also a letter of commendation from the Abuna. An escort of soldiers was offered us, but refused. The expedition consisted simply of ourselves, a bullet-headed Armenian chauffeur, and a small native boy, who attached himself to us without invitation. At first we were a little resentful of this, but he firmly refused to understand our attempts at dismissal, and later we were devoutly grateful for his presence. The car, which did things I should have thought no car could possibly do, was an American make which is rarely seen in Europe. When we had packed it with our overcoats, rugs, tins of petrol, and provisions, there was just room for ourselves. The hotel supplied beer and sandwiches and olives and oranges, and Irene gave us a hamper of tinned and truffled foods from Fortnum & Mason. We were just starting, rather later than we had hoped, when Professor W. remembered something. 'Do you mind if we go back to my hotel for a minute? There's just one thing I've forgotten.' We drove round to the Imperial.

The thing he had forgotten was a dozen empty Vichy-bottles. 'I thought it would be courteous,' he explained, 'to take some holy water back to Ras Kassa and the Abuna. I'm sure they would appreciate it.'

'Yes, but need we take quite so much?'

'Well, there's the patriarchal legate, I should like to give him some, and Belatingeta Herui, and the Coptic patriarch at Cairo . . . I thought it was a nice opportunity to repay some of the kindness I have received.'

I suggested that this purpose could be more conveniently achieved by giving them *tedj*, and that from what I had seen of Abyssinians they would much prefer it. Professor W. gave a little nervous laugh and looked anxiously out of the window.

'Well, why not fill my empty beer-bottles?'

'No, no, I don't think that would be quite suitable. I don't really like using Vichy-bottles. I wish I had had time to scrape off the labels,' he mused. 'I don't *quite* like the idea of holy water in Vichy-bottles. Perhaps the boy could do it tomorrow – before they are filled, of course.'

A new aspect of the professor's character was thus revealed. My acquaintance with him until that day was limited to half a dozen more or less casual encounters at the various parties and shows. I had found him full of agreeably ironical criticism of our companions, very punctilious, and very enthusiastic about things which seemed to me unexceptionable. 'Look,' he would say with purest Boston intonation, 'look at the exquisite grace of the basket that woman is carrying. There is the whole character of the people in that plaited straw. Ah, why do we waste our time looking at crowns and canons? I could study that basket all day.' And a wistful, faraway look would come into his eyes as he spoke.

Remarks of that kind went down very well with some people, and I regarded them as being, perhaps, one of the normal manifestations of American scholarship. They were compensated for by such sound maxims as 'Never carry binoculars; you only have to hand them over to some wretched woman as soon as there is anything worth seeing.' But this worldly good sense was a mere mask over the essential mystical nature of the professor's mind; one touch of church furniture, and he became suddenly transfused with reverence and an almost neurotic eagerness to do all that could be expected of him, with an impulsive and demonstrative devotion that added a great deal to the glamour of our expedition together.

Those bottles, however, were an infernal nuisance. They clinked about the floor, making all the difference between tolerable ease and acute discomfort. There was nowhere to rest our feet except on their unstable, rolling surface. We drew up our knees and resigned ourselves to cramp and pins and needles.

Debra Lebanos is practically due north of Addis Ababa. For the first mile or two there was a clearly marked track which led out of the town, right over the summit of Entoto. It was extremely steep and narrow, composed of loose stones and boulders; on the top of the hill was a little church and parsonage, the ground all round them broken by deep ravines and outcrops of stone. 'Whatever happens,' we decided, 'we must make quite certain of coming over here by daylight.'

From Entoto the way led down to a wide plain, watered

by six or seven shallow streams which flowed between deep banks at right angles to our road. Caravans of mules were coming into the town laden with skins. Professor W. saluted them with bows and blessings; the hillmen answered him with blank stares or broad incredulous grins. A few, more sophisticated than their companions, bellowed, 'Baksheesh!' Professor W. shook his head sadly and remarked that the people were already getting spoiled by foreign intrusion.

It took two or three hours to cross the plain; we drove, for the most part, parallel to the track, rather than on it, finding the rough ground more comfortable than the pre-pared surface. We crossed numerous dry watercourses and several streams. At some of these there had been rough attempts at bridge-building, usually a heap of rocks and a few pieces of timber; in rare cases a culvert ran underneath. It was in negotiating these that we first realised the aston-ishing powers of our car. It would plunge nose first into a precipitous gully, shiver and stagger a little, churn up dust and stones, roar, and skid, bump and sway until we began to climb out, and then it would suddenly start forward and mount very deliberately up the other side as though endowed with some peculiar prehensile quality in its tyres. Occasion-ally, in conditions of scarcely conceivable asperity, the engine would stop. Professor W. would sigh and open the door, allowing two or three of his empty bottles to roll out on to the running-board.

'Ah, ça n'a pas d'importance,' said the driver, prodding the boy, who jumped out, restored the bottles, and then leant his shoulder against the back of the car. This infinitesimal contribution of weight seemed to be all the car needed; up it would go out of the river-bed, and over the crest of the bank, gaining speed as it reached level ground; the child would race after us and clamber in as we bumped along, a triumphant smile on his little black face.

At about eleven we stopped for luncheon by the side of the last stream. The boy busied himself by filling up the radiator by the use of a small cup. I ate sandwiches and drank beer rendered volatile by the motion of the car. The professor turned out to be a vegetarian; he unwrapped a little segment of cheese from its silver paper and nibbled it delicately and made a very neat job of an orange. The sun was very powerful, and the professor advanced what seemed, and still seems, to me the radically unsound theory that you must wear thick woollen underclothes if you wish to keep cool in the tropics.

After leaving the plain we drove for three hours or so across grassy downland. There was now no track of any kind, but occasional boundary-stones hinted at the way we should follow. There were herds grazing, usually in the charge of small naked children. At first the professor politely raised his hat and bowed to them, but the effect was so disturbing that after he had sent three or four out of sight, wailing in terror, he remarked that it was agreeable to find people who had a proper sense of the menace of motor transport, and relapsed into meditation, pondering, perhaps, the advisability of presenting a little holy water to the emperor. The route was uneventful, broken only by occasional clusters of *tukals*, surrounded by high hedges of euphorbia. It was very hot, and after a time, in spite of the jangle of the bottles and the constriction of space, I fell into a light doze.

I awoke as we stopped on the top of a hill; all round us were empty undulations of grass. 'Nous sommes perdus?' asked the professor. 'Ça n'a pas d'importance,' replied the driver, lighting a cigarette. The boy was dispatched, like the dove from Noah's ark, to find direction in the void. We waited for half an hour before he returned. Meanwhile three native women appeared from nowhere, peering at us from under straw sunshades. The professor took off his hat and bowed. The women huddled together and giggled. Presently fascination overcame their shyness and they approached closer; one touched the radiator and burned her fingers. They asked for cigarettes and were repelled, with some very forceful language, by the driver.

At last the child returned and made some explanations. We turned off at right angles and drove on, and the professor and I fell asleep once more.

When I next woke, the landscape had changed dramatically. About half a mile from us, and obliquely to the line of our path, the ground fell away suddenly into a great canyon. I do not know how deep it was, but I should think at least two thousand feet, descending abruptly in tiers of sheer cliff, broken by strips and patches of timber. At the bottom a river ran between green banks, to swell the Blue Nile far in the south; it was practically dry at this season except for a few shining channels of water which split and reunited on the sandy bed in delicate threads of light. Poised among trees, two-thirds of the way down on a semi-circular shelf of land, we could discern the roofs of Debra Lebanos. A cleft path led down the face of the cliff and it was for this that we were clearly making. It looked hopelessly unsafe, but our Armenian plunged down with fine intrepidity.

Sometimes we lurched along a narrow track with cliffs rising on one side and a precipice falling away on the other; sometimes we picked our way on broad ledges among great volcanic boulders; sometimes we grated between narrow rock walls. At last we reached a defile which even our driver admitted to be impassable. We climbed out along the running-boards and finished the descent on foot. Professor W. was clearly already enchanted by the sanctity of the place.

'Look,' he said, pointing to some columns of smoke that rose from the cliffs above us, 'the cells of the solitary anchorites.'

'Are you sure there are solitary anchorites here? I never heard of any.'

'It would be a good place for them,' he said wistfully.

The Armenian strode on in front of us, a gallant little fig-ure with his cropped head and rotund, gaitered legs; the boy staggered behind, carrying overcoats, blankets, provisions, and a good half-dozen of the empty bottles. Suddenly the Armenian stopped and, with his finger on his lips, drew our attention to the rocks just below us. Twenty or thirty baboons of both sexes and all ages were huddled up in the shade.

'Ah,' said Professor W., 'sacred monkeys. How very inter-esting!'

'Why do you think they are sacred? They seem perfectly wild.'

'It is a common thing to find sacred monkeys in monas-teries,' he explained gently. 'I have seen them in Ceylon and in many parts of India . . . Oh, why did he have to do that? How very thoughtless!' For our driver had throne a stone into their midst and scattered them barking in all directions, to the great delight of the small boy behind us.

It was hot walking. We passed one or two *tukals* with women and children staring curiously at us, and eventually emerged on to an open green ledge littered with enormous rocks and a variety of unimposing buildings. A mob of ragged boys, mostly infected with disagreeable skin diseases, surrounded us and were repelled by the Armenian. (These, we learned later, were the deacons.) We sent the boy forward to find someone more responsible, and soon a fine-looking, bearded monk, carrying a yellow sunshade, came out of the shadow of a tree

and advanced to greet us. We gave him our letter of introduction from the Abuna, and after he had scrutinised both
sides of the envelope with some closeness, he agreed,
through our Armenian, who from now on acted as interpreter, to fetch the head of the monastery. He was away some
time and eventually returned with an old priest, who wore
a brown cloak, a very large white turban, steel-rimmed spectacles, and carried in one hand an old black umbrella and in
the other a horsehair fly-whisk. Professor W. darted forward
and kissed the cross which swung from the old man's neck.
This was received rather well, but I felt too shy to follow his
lead and contented myself with shaking hands. The monk
then handed his superior our letter, which was tucked away
in his pocket unopened. They then explained that they would
be ready to receive us shortly, and went off to wake up the
other priests and prepare the chapter house.

We waited about half an hour, sitting in the shade near
the church, and gradually forming round us a circle of
inquisitive ecclesiastics of all ages. The Armenian went off to
see about his car. Professor W. replied to the questions that
were put to us, with bows, shakes of the head, and little sympathetic moans. Presently one monk came up and, squatting
beside us, began to write on the back of his hand with a
white pencil in a regular, finely formed Amharic script. One
of the letters was in the form of a cross. Professor W., anxious to inform them all that we were good Christians,

pointed to this mark, then to me and to himself, bowed in the direction of the church, and crossed himself. This time he made a less happy impression. Everyone looked bewildered and rather scared; the scribe spat on his hand, and hastily erasing the text, fell back some paces. There was an air of tension and embarrassment, which was fortunately disturbed by our Armenian with the announcement that the council of the monastery were now ready to receive us.

Apart from the two churches, the most prominent building was a tall, square house of stone, with a thatched roof and a single row of windows set high up under the eaves; it was here that we were led. A small crowd had collected round the door, which was covered with a double curtain of heavy sackcloth. The windows also were heavily screened, so that we stepped from the brilliant sunshine into a gloom which was at first completely baffling. One of the priests raised the door-curtain a little to show us our way. A single lofty room constituted the entire house; the walls were of undisguised stone and rubble, no ceiling covered the rafters and thatch. Preparations had clearly been made for us; carpets had been spread on the earthen floor, and in the centre stood two low stools covered with rugs; twelve priests stood ranged against the wall, the head of the monastery in their centre; between them and our seats stood a table covered with a shawl; the only other furniture was a cupboard in the far corner, roughly built of irregularly stained white wood, the doors secured with a staple and padlock. We sat down and our chauffeur-interpreter stood beside us jauntily twirling his cap. When we were settled, the head of the monastery, who apparently also bore the title of abuna, brought our letter of introduction out of his pocket and, for the first time, opened it. He read it first to himself and then aloud to the company, who scratched their beards, nodded, and grunted. Then he addressed us, asking us what we wanted. Professor W. explained that we had heard from afar of the sanctity of the place and the wisdom and piety of the monks, and that we had come to do reverence at their shrine, pay our duty and respect to them, and take away some account of the glories of the monastery of which all the world stood in awe. This pretty speech was condensed by our chauffeur into three or four harsh vocables, and greeted with further nods and grunts from the assembly.

One of them asked whether we were Mohammedans. It seemed sad that this question was necessary after all Professor W.'s protestations. We assured him that we were not. Another asked where we had come from. Addis Ababa? They asked about the coronation, and Professor W. began a graphic outline of the liturgical significance of the ceremony. I do not think, however, that our chauffeur was at very great pains to translate this faithfully. The response, anyway, was a general outburst of chuckling, and from then onwards, for about ten minutes, he took the burden of conversation from our shoulders and speedily established relations of the utmost geniality. Presently he began shaking hands with them all and explained that they would like us to do the same, a social duty which Professor W. decorated with many graceful genuflections and reverences.

The professor then asked whether we might visit the library of which the world stood in awe. Why, certainly; there it was in the corner. The abuna produced a small key from his pocket and directed one of the priests to open the cupboard. They brought out five or six bundles wrapped in silk shawls, and, placing them with great care on the table, drew back the door-curtain to admit a shaft of white light. The abuna lifted the corners of the shawls one after another and revealed two pieces of board clumsily hinged together in the form of a diptych. Professor W. kissed them eagerly; they were then opened, revealing two coloured lithographs, apparently cut from a religious almanac printed in Germany some time towards the end of the last century, representing the Crucifixion and the Assumption, pasted on to the inner surfaces of the wood. The professor was clearly a little taken aback. 'Dear, dear, how remarkably ugly they are,' he remarked as he bent down to kiss them.

The other bundles contained manuscripts of the Gospels, lives of the saints, and missals, written in Ghiz[1] and brightly

---

1. The ecclesiastical language, unintelligible to all the laity and most of the priesthood. It is written in Amharic characters.

illuminated. The painting was of the same kind as the frescos, reduced to miniature. Sometimes faces and figures had
been cut out of prints and stuck into the pages with a dis-
composing effect on their highly stylised surroundings. They
told us with great pride that the artist had been employed at
Addis Ababa on some work for the late empress. Professor
W. asked whether there were not some older manuscripts
we might see, but they affected not to understand. I remembered hearing from George Herui that it was only after very
considerable difficulties that Professor Mercer had unearthed
his Ecclesiastes. No doubt there were still reserves hidden
from us.

It was then suggested that we should visit the sacred
spring. Our Armenian here sidled unobtrusively out of the
way; he had had enough exercise for one day. Professor W.
and I set out with a guide up the hillside. It was a stiff climb;
the sun was still strong and the stones all radiated a fierce
heat. 'I think, perhaps, we ought to take off our hats,' said the
professor; 'we are on very holy ground.'

I removed my topi and exposed myself to sunstroke, trust-
ing in divine protection; but, just as he spoke, it so happened
that our guide stopped on the path and accommodated himself in a way which made me think that his reverence for the
spot was far from fanatical.

On our way we passed a place where overhanging cliffs
formed a shallow cave. Water oozed and dripped all round,

and the path was soft and slippery. It is here that the bodies of the faithful are brought; they lay all about, some in packing-cases, others in hollow tree trunks, battened down with planks, piled and tumbled on top of each other without order; many were partially submerged in falls of damp earth, a few of these rough coffins had broken apart, revealing their contents. There were similar heaps, we were told, on the other parts of the hillside.

We had a fine view of the valley; our guide pointed out a group of buildings on the far side. 'That is the convent for the women,' he explained. 'You see it is quite untrue that we live together. The houses are entirely separate. We do not cross the valley to see them, and they do not cross to us. Never. It is all a lie.' He wanted to make this point quite clear.

At last we reached the spring, which fell in a pretty cas-cade to join the river far below at the bottom of the valley. Most of the water, however, had been tapped, and was con-veyed in two iron pipes to bathing-places near the monastery. We climbed down again to see them. One, built especially for Menelik, was a little brick house with a corrugated-iron roof. The old empress had frequently come here, and since her death it had not been used. We peered through the win-dow and saw a plain kitchen-chair. There was a rusty spout in the ceiling from which a trickle of water fell on to the brick floor and drained away through the waste-pipe in one corner. The other bath was for public use. The pipe was fitted with a double spout, directing two streams of water on to either side of a brick wall. One side was for men and the other for women, and a three-sided screen was built round each. The floor was made of cement. A boy was in there at the time of our visit, swilling himself down with as much puffing and spluttering as if he were under any purely secular shower-bath.

As we turned back, our Armenian and a monk met us with a message from the abuna – should they kill a goat, a sheep, or a calf for our dinner? We explained that we had full provision for our food. All we required was shelter for the night and water to wash in. The Armenian explained that it was usual to accept something. We suggested some eggs, but were told that they had none. They urged a goat very strongly. Meat is a rare luxury in the monastery, and they were, no doubt, eager to take the opportunity of our visit for a feast. The professor's vegetarian scruples, however, were unconquerable. At last they suggested honey, which he accepted readily. The question of our accommodation was then discussed. There was a hut or a tent. The Armenian warned us that if we slept in the hut we should certainly contract some repulsive disease, and if in the tent, we might be killed by hyenas. He had already made up his own mind, he said, to sleep in the car. We returned to the monastery, and the abuna led us in person to see the hut. It was some time before the key could be found; when the door was at last wrenched

open, an emaciated she-goat ran out. The interior was windowless and fetid. It appeared to have been used as a kind of
lumber-room; heaps of old rags and broken furniture
encumbered the floor. A swarm of bees buzzed in the roof.
It was not quite ready, the abuna explained; he had not
expected guests. It could, of course, be prepared, or would
we think it inhospitable if he offered us the tent? We declared
that the tent would be wholly satisfactory, and so, with evident relief, the abuna gave instructions for its erection. It was
now nearly sunset. A spot of ground was chosen near the
house where we had been received, and a very decent bell-
tent pitched. (It was the property of the old empress, we
learned. She had often slept there on her visits to the spring.)
The floor was covered with hay and the hay with rugs. A little
boat-shaped oil-lamp was hung from the tent-pole; our rugs,
provisions, and bottles were brought in and laid on one side.
We were then invited to enter. We sat down cross-legged and
the abuna sat beside us. He looked enormous in the tiny
light; the shadow from his great turban seemed to fill the
whole tent. The chauffeur squatted opposite us. The abuna
smiled with the greatest geniality and expressed his best
wishes for our comfort; we thanked him heartily. Conversation lapsed and we all three sat smiling rather vacantly.
Presently the flap was lifted and a monk came in wearing a
heavy brown burnous and carrying an antiquated rifle. He
bowed to us and retired. He was a guard, the abuna explained,

who would sleep outside across the door. Another smiling pause. At last supper arrived; first a basket containing half a dozen great rounds of native bread, a tough, clammy substance closely resembling crêpe rubber in appearance; then two earthenware jugs, one of water, the other of *talla* – a kind of thin, bitter beer; then two horns of honey, but not of honey as it is understood at Thame; this was the product of wild bees, scraped straight from the trees; it was a greyish colour, full of bits of stick and mud, bird dung, dead bees, and grubs. Everything was first carried to the abuna for his approval, then to us. We expressed our delight with nods and more extravagant smiles. The food was laid out before us and the bearers retired. At this moment the Armenian shamelessly deserted us, saying that he must go and see after his boy.

The three of us were left alone, smiling over our food in the half darkness.

In the corner lay our hamper packed with Irene's European delicacies. We clearly could not approach them until our host left us. Gradually the frightful truth became evident that he was proposing to dine with us. I tore off a little rag of bread and attempted to eat it. 'This is a very difficult situation,' said the professor; 'I think, perhaps, it would be well to simulate ill-health,' and holding his hands to his forehead, he began to rock gently from side to side, emitting painfully subdued moans. It was admirably done; the abuna watched him with the greatest concern; presently the professor held his stomach and retched a little; then he lay on his back, breathing heavily with closed eyes; then he sat up on his elbow and explained in eloquent dumb show that he wished to rest. The abuna understood perfectly, and, with every gesture of sympathy, rose to his feet and left us.

In five minutes, when I had opened a tinned grouse and a bottle of lager and the professor was happily munching a handful of ripe olives, the Armenian returned. With a comprehensive wink, he picked up the jug of native beer, threw back his head, and, without pausing to breathe, drank a quart or two. He then spread out two rounds of bread, emptied a large quantity of honey into each of them, wrapped them together, and put them in his pocket. 'Moi, je puis manger comme abyssin,' he remarked cheerfully, winked at the grouse, wished us good night, and left us.

'Now at last,' said the professor, producing a tin of Keating's powder, 'I feel in the heart of Ethiopia.' He sprinkled the rugs and blankets, wrapped his head in a pale grey scarf, and prepared to settle down for the night. We had had a tiring day, and after smoking a pipe I decided to follow his example. The lamp was flickering and smoking badly and threatened at any moment to burn through its own string and set us on fire. I blew it out, and was just becoming drowsy when the abuna returned, carrying a lantern, to see whether the professor felt any better. We all smiled inarticulately for some time, and the professor pointed to the half-empty beer-jug and the horns of honey as proof of his recovery. The abuna noted them with evident satisfaction, and then his eye, travelling round the tent, was attracted by the Keating's powder which lay like thick dust over the floor and bedding. He called in the guard and rather crossly pointed out this evidence of neglect. The man hastily produced a broom and brushed out the tent. Then, when everything was in order, and after many bows, smiles, and blessings, he left us to sleep.

But I, at any rate, slept very little. It was a deadly cold night and a bitter wind sprang up, sweeping the valley and driving under the tent and through our thin blankets, while outside the door the guard coughed and grunted. I was out before dawn and watched the monastery waking into life. There seemed very little order. The monks emerged from the huts in ones and twos and pottered off to work in the fields and woods. A certain number of them went down to the church, where the professor and I followed them. They sat about outside until a priest appeared with the keys; then a service began, apparently quite at haphazard. Two or three would start intoning some kind of psalm or litany, and others seemed to join in as they thought fit; two or three were reading aloud from large manuscripts supported on folding rests; others leant on their praying-sticks or squatted in corners muttering. Now and then one would stop on his way to work, kiss the door on the inner wall, and pass on. The frescos of the inner sanctuary were hung with green curtains; one of the priests pointed to them and explained in dumb show that they would be drawn for our inspection later in the day.

We returned to our tent for breakfast. Beer and anchovies seemed rather discouraging after our chilly night, but there was no alternative except tinned loganberries and *foie gras*. The guard came in, finished the beer, and ate some bread and honey. He showed great interest in our belongings, fingering everything in turn – the tin-opener, electric torch, a pocket-knife, a pair of hairbrushes. I let him play with the sword-stick I happened to have brought with me; he in exchange showed me his rifle and bandoleer. About half the cartridges were empty shells; the weapon was in very poor condition. It could not possibly have been used with any accuracy, and probably not with safety. I asked whether he had ever killed anything with it; he shook his head, and produced a large, rather blunt dagger, which he stabbed into the earth.

Presently the chauffeur came to assure us that he had spent a very comfortable night and felt fairly confident that he would be able to extricate the car from its position on the path, where it blocked all approach to the monastery and was causing a good deal of trouble to the herdsmen in charge of the community's cattle. We told him to remain at hand to act as interpreter, and soon a priest came to conduct us to the churches. There were two of these; the main building, where we had already been, and a small shrine, containing a cross which had fallen from heaven. The professor thought this might be a piece of the true cross brought there from Alexandria after the Arab invasion, and showed great interest and veneration; we were not allowed to see it, but as a special concession we were shown the shawl in which it was wrapped.

In the main church we paid a fee of seven dollars to have the frescos unveiled. They had lately been repainted in brilliant colours and the priest was justly proud of the renovation. On one wall were portraits of Ras Kassa, Menelik, and the late empress. It was clear that these heads had been copied from photographs, with the curious result that they stood out solidly, in carefully articulated light and shade and great fidelity of detail, against a composition of purely conventional pre-Renaissance design. Another wall was filled with rider saints. The professor made a plan of it and took down their names. We were then shown some brass processional crosses and some illuminated missals, none of any great antiquity. It was, in fact, a curious feature of Debra Lebanos that, although the community had been the centre of Abyssinian spiritual life since very early days in the conversion of the country, and had been settled on this spot for several centuries, they seem to have preserved no single object from the past. It may be that their treasures have all been pillaged in the continual invasions and disorders of

Abyssinian history, or that they have been sold from time to time in moments of financial need, or perhaps simply that they did not choose to show them to strangers.

One thing, however, we did see of the greatest interest. That was the sanctuary. We might not, of course, enter it, but the priest drew back the curtain for us and allowed a short glimpse of the dark interior. In the centre stood the tabot, which is both altar-stone and tabernacle, a wooden cupboard built like a miniature church in three tiers, square at the base, from which rose an octagonal storey surmounted by a circular dome. Round the tabot, in deep dust, for the sanctuary is rarely, if ever, swept out, lay an astonishing confusion of litter. There was no time to take in everything, but, in the brief inspection, I noticed a wicker chair, some heaps of clothes, two or three umbrellas, a suitcase of imitation leather, some newspapers, and a teapot and slop-pail of enamelled tin.

It was about ten o'clock when we left the church; there was a Mass at one o'clock, which we were both anxious to attend, which would not be over until half-past two or three. We were thus undecided about our movements. We might spend another night there and start back early next day for Addis Ababa; we might go and see Fiche, Kassa's capital fifteen miles away, and spend a night in the car there, or we might start immediately after Mass and try to get to Addis that night. The chauffeur favoured the last plan and was hopeful of his ability, now that he knew the way, of doing the journey in five or six hours. We had not provisions to last us in any comfort for two days, and I was reluctant to fall back on Abyssinian food. Together we persuaded the professor to attempt the journey; if the worst came to the worst we could spend the night on the plain; a prospect to which the chauffeur added romance with gloomy stories of wild beasts and brigands. As the sun mounted, it became intensely hot. We lay in the tent smoking and dozing until the abuna came to conduct us to Mass.

I will not attempt any description of the ritual; the liturgy was quite unintelligible to me, and, oddly enough, to the professor also. No doubt the canon of the Mass would have been in part familiar, but this was said in the sanctuary behind closed doors. We stood in the outer ambulatory. A carpet was placed for us to stand on and we were given praying-sticks, with the aid of which we stood throughout the two hours of service. There were twenty or thirty monks round us and some women and babies from the *tukals*. Communion was administered to the babies, but to no one else. Many of the monks were crippled or deformed in some way; presumably they were pilgrims who had originally come to the spring in the hope of a cure, and had become absorbed into the life of the place. There seemed to be very little system of testing vocations in the community. The priests and deacons wore long, white-and-gold cloaks and turbans, and had bare feet. Now and then they emerged from the sanctuary, and once they walked round in procession. The singing was monotonous and more or less continuous, accompanied by a drum and sistrums.[1] For anyone accustomed to the Western rite it was difficult to think of this as a Christian service, for it bore that secret and confused character which I had hitherto associated with the non-Christian sects of the East.

I had sometimes thought it an odd thing that Western Christianity, alone of all the religions of the world, exposes its mysteries to every observer, but I was so accustomed to this openness that I had never before questioned whether it was an essential and natural feature of the Christian system. Indeed, so saturated are we in this spirit that many people regard the growth of the Church as a process of elaboration − even of obfuscation; they visualise the Church of the first century as a little cluster of pious people reading the Gospels together, praying and admonishing each other with a simplicity to which the high ceremonies and subtle theology of later years would have been bewildering and unrecognisable. At Debra Lebanos I suddenly saw the classic basilica and open altar as a great positive achievement, a triumph of light over darkness consciously accomplished, and I saw theology as the science of simplification by which nebulous and elusive ideas are formalised and made intelli-

1. Silver rattles.

gible and exact. I saw the Church of the first century as a dark and hidden thing, as dark and hidden as the seed germinating in the womb; legionaries off duty slipping furtively out of barracks, greeting each other by signs and passwords in a locked upper room in the side street of some Mediterranean sea port; slaves at dawn creeping from the grey twilight into the candle-lit, smoky chapels of the catacombs. The priests hid their office, practising trades; their identity was known only to initiates; they were criminals against the law of their country. And the pure nucleus of the truth lay in the minds of the people, encumbered with superstitions, gross survivals of the paganism in which they had been brought up; hazy and obscene nonsense seeping through from the other esoteric cults of the Near East, magical infections from the conquered barbarian. And I began to see how these obscure sanctuaries had grown, with the clarity of the Western reason, into the great open altars of Catholic Europe, where Mass is said in a flood of light, high in the sight of all, while tourists can clatter around with their Baedekers, incurious of the mystery.

By the time Mass was over, our chauffeur had succeeded in the remarkable and hazardous feat of backing the car up the path. We said good-bye to the abuna and climbed the ravine, attended by a troop of small deacons. When we at last reached the top the professor took from his pocket a handful of half-piastre pieces with which he had secretly provided himself. He ordered the children to line up, and our boy cuffed and jostled them into some kind of order. Then he presented them with a coin apiece. They had clearly not expected any such donation, but they quickly got the hang of the business, and, as soon as they were paid, queued up again at the back. Our boy detected this simple deception and drove away the second-comers. When each had received his half-piastre, and some had grabbed two, there were still a number of coins left over. 'Do you think,' asked the professor rather timidly, 'that it would be very vulgar and tripperish to make them scramble for them?'

'Yes,' I said.

'Of course it would,' said the professor decidedly. 'Quite out of the question.'

The deacons, however, continued to caper round us, crying for more and clinging to the car, so that it became impossible to start without endangering several lives. 'Ça n'a pas d'importance,' said the chauffeur inevitably, cranking up the engine. The professor, however, preferred a more humane release. 'Perhaps, after all . . .' he said, and threw his handful of money among the children. The last we saw of Debra Lebanos was a scrambling of naked black limbs and a cloud of dust. It was interesting to be in at the birth of a tradition. Whoever in future goes to Debra Lebanos will, without doubt, find himself beset by these rapacious children; Professor W. had taught them the first easy lesson of civilisation. It is curious how

Americans, however cultured, seem incapable of neglecting this form of instruction.

Our journey back for the first three hours was uneventful. We made good time on the downs, and darkness found us at the beginning of the plain. From then onwards progress was slow and uncertain. Four or five times we lost the track and continued out of our way until a patch of bush or marsh brought us up short. Twice we got stuck and had to push our way out; two or three times we were nearly overturned by sudden subsidences into the watercourses. It was these channels that enabled us to find our way, for they all ran at right angles to our route. When we reached one the Armenian and the boy would take opposite sides and follow the bank down until one of them reached the crossing; there would then be whistles and signals and we resumed the right road.

At each check, the professor made up his mind to stop. 'It is quite impossible. We shall never find the road until daylight. We may be going miles out of our way. It is dangerous and futile. We had far better spend the night here and go back at dawn.'

Then the driver would return with news of success. 'J'ai décidé; nous arrêtons ici,' the professor would say.

'Ah,' came the invariable response, 'vous savez, monsieur, ça n'a pas d'importance.'

Throughout the journey the boy sat on the mudguard in front, picking out the rare stones and hoof-marks which directed us. Once, however, the Armenian despaired. We had all walked round and round for half an hour in widening circles, searching the completely blank earth with electric torches. We came back defeated. It was now about ten o'clock and bitterly cold. We were just discussing how we could possibly keep ourselves warm during the coming eight hours, when the boy saw lights ahead. We drove on and ran straight into a caravan bivouacked round a campfire. Our arrival caused great consternation in the camp. Men and women ran out of the tents or sprang out of the ground from huddled heaps of blankets; the animals sprang up and strained at their tethers or tumbled about with hobbled legs. Rifles were levelled at us. The Armenian strode into their midst, however, and, after distributing minute sums of money as a sign of goodwill, elicited directions.

Our worst check was within sight of Addis, on the top of Entoto. This part of the journey had seemed perilous enough by daylight, but by now we were so stiff and cold as to be indifferent to any other consideration. Twice we pulled up within a few feet of the precipice, the boy having fallen asleep on the mudguard where he sat. We got stuck again with two wheels in the air and two in a deep gully, but eventually we found the road and at that moment ran out of petrol. Two minutes earlier this disaster would have been insuperable. From now on, however, it was all downhill, and we ran into the town without the engine. When at last we reached the professor's hotel we were too tired to say good night. He silently picked up his bottles of holy water and, with a little nod, went up to his room, and I had fallen asleep before he was out of sight. A sulky night-porter found us a can of petrol and we drove on to the Hôtel de France. The manager was sitting up for me with a boiling kettle and a bottle of rum. I slept well that night.

Five

In London, full of ingenuous eagerness to get aboard, I had booked my ticket through to Zanzibar, between which island and Djibouti the Messageries Maritimes maintain a fortnightly service. Now, with everyone else going home, I began to rather regret the arrangement and think wistfully of an Irish Christmas. The next ship, the *Général Voyson*, was not due for ten days, and the prospect of spending the time either at Addis Ababa or Djibouti was unattractive. The difficulty (and of course the charm) of Abyssinia is the inaccessibility of the interior. I should dearly have liked to make a journey north to Axum or Lallibella, but this would require camping-equipment and the organisation of a caravan; it would take many weeks and more money than I could conveniently afford; even so, I would have attempted it if I had been able to find a companion, but no one seemed ready to come, and it seemed futile to set out alone in complete ignorance of the geography and language of the country. I was on the point of forfeiting my ticket and joining the Italian ship by which Irene was sailing north, when Mr Plowman, the Brit-ish consul at Harar, who with his family was visiting the capital for the coronation, very kindly suggested that I should return with him and break my journey at his home for a few days. No suggestion could have been more delightful. There was glamour in all the associations of Harar, the Arab city-state which stood first among the fruits of Ethiopian imperialism, the scene of Sir Richard Burton's *First Steps in Africa*, the market where the caravans met between coast and highlands; where Galla, Somali, and Arab interbred to produce women whose beauty was renowned throughout East Africa. There is talk of a motor-road that is to connect it with the railway, but at present it must still be approached by the tortuous hill-pass and small track along which Arthur Rimbaud had sent rifles to Menelik.

Except for one overpowering afternoon spent scrambling with Irene through the forest of Jemjem in hopeless pursuit of black-and-white monkeys, the last days before we left Addis were agreeably quiet and enabled us to readjust our rather feverish impressions of the town and its inhabitants. On the morning of November 15th we left by the last of the special trains. The departure took place with far less formality than the arrivals. There was no band, but the platform was crowded with the whole European population. Even our Armenian chauffeur came to see us off; the carriage in which I travelled was filled with little bunches of flowers hung there by the servants of one of the British officials who was going home on leave. Mr Hall was there with eye-glass and top hat.

He trusted that anything I wrote about Abyssinia would be friendly and sympathetic. I assured him that it would be so.

Next day at dawn we arrived at Dirre-Dowa, and the Plowmans and I took leave of our fellow passengers. We had all spent a practically sleepless night, and for the greater part of that hot Sunday we remained in our rooms at Bollolakos' hotel. I went to Mass at a church full of odious French children, washed in a sandy bath, slept, and wrote an article on Abyssinian politics to post to my paper. As I sealed up the envelope I had the agreeable feeling of being once more a free man. I could now come and go as I liked. I could meet people without seeing in their eye the embarrassed consciousness that they were talking to 'the Press'; it affected people in various ways, some were reticent to the verge of rudeness, others so expansive as to be almost tedious, but no one, I found, treated a journalist quite as a fellow human being.

We dined that evening in a pleasant little party consisting of the Plowmans and their governess, the Cypriot manager of the local bank, Mr Hall's brother, who was in business at Dirre-Dowa, and his wife, an English lady who wore a large enamelled brooch made in commemoration of the opening of Epping Forest to the public and presented to her father who was, at the time, an alderman of the City of London. We sat in the open under an orange-tree and drank chianti and gossiped about the coronation, while many hundreds of small red ants overran the table and fell on to our heads from above.

The Plowmans' horses had not arrived that day, so that their start would have to be delayed until Tuesday morning and their arrival at Harar until Thursday. The director of the railway had wired to the station-master at Dirre-Dowa to reserve mules and servants for me, and I decided to avail myself of them next day and reach Harar a day ahead of my hosts. I felt that it was, in a way, more suitable to enter the town alone and unofficially.

Accordingly, I set out early next morning, riding a lethargic grey mule, accompanied by a mounted Abyssinian guide who spoke French, an aged groom who attached himself to me against my express orders, and a Galla porter, of singularly villainous expression, to carry my luggage. We had not been going long before this man, easily out-distancing our beasts, disappeared into the hills with great lurching strides, the bag containing my passport, letter of credit, and all of my essential clothes balanced negligently on his head. I became apprehensive, and the guide was anything but reassuring. All Gallas were dishonest, he explained, and this one was a particularly dirty type. He disclaimed all responsibility for engaging him; that had been done by the station-master; he himself would never have chosen a man of such obvious criminal characteristics. It was not unusual for porters to desert with the luggage; there was no catching them once they got over the hills among their own people; they had murdered an Indian not long ago in circumstances of peculiar atrocity. But it was possible, he added, that the man had merely hurried on to take his *khat*.[1]

This was, in fact, what had happened. We came upon him again some hours later, squatting by the roadside with his lap full of the leaves and his teeth and mouth green with chewing; his expression had softened considerably under the influence of the drug, and for the rest of the journey he was docile enough, trailing along behind us in a slightly bemused condition.

For the first few miles we followed the river-bed, a broad stretch of sand which for a few hours in the year is flooded from bank to bank with a turgid mountain torrent, which sweeps down timber and boulders and carries away the accumulated refuse of the town. It was now nearing the end of the dry season and the way was soft and powdery; it was heavy going until we reached the foot of the caravan route. There is a short cut over the hills which is used by foot passengers and riders who are much pressed for time; on the guide's advice we chose the longer and more leisurely road

1. This is a herb of mildly intoxicating properties eaten extensively by Arabs and the Mohammedan peoples of East Africa. Its effect is temporarily stimulating, but enervating in the long run. Habitual *khat* chewers are said to be more satisfactory as workmen, but less satisfactory as husbands. It is bitter in taste, rather like sorrel. I ate a leaf or two without noticing any effect; the real addict browses every morning on a great bundle.

which winds in a long detour round the spur and joins the rock path at the summit. It is about four hours from the hotel to the uplands by this road. The mules took things easily; it was necessary to beat them more or less continually to keep them moving at all. At the top we paused for a rest.

Behind us, as far as we could see, the country was utterly desolate; the hillside up which we had climbed was covered with colourless sand and rock, and beyond, on the other side of the valley, rose other hills equally bare of dwelling or cultivation. The only sign of life was a caravan of camels, roped nose to tail, following us a mile or so below. In front of us everything was changed. This was Galla country, full of little villages and roughly demarcated arable plots. The road in places was bordered with cactus and flowering euphorbia-trees; the air was fresh and vital.

Another three hours brought us to a native inn, where the boys hoped to get some food. The landlord, however, told us that the local governor had recently cancelled his licence, an injustice which he attributed to the rivalry of the Greek who kept the rest house at Haramaya. He provided them with a tin can full of talla, which the two Christians drank; the Mohammedan religiously contenting himself with another handful of khat. Then we went on. In another four hours we were in sight of the lake of Haramaya, a welcoming sheet of light between two green hills. It was here that we proposed to break the journey for a night. It is not difficult to ride through in one day on a pony; it is quite possible on a mule, but most people prefer to wait until the next morning. It is another four hours on, and four hours at that stage seem barely supportable. Moreover, the gates of the city are shut at sundown and it is sometimes difficult to obtain admission after that time. I was tired out, and at the sight of water the mules for the first time showed some sign of interest. Indeed, it became impossible to keep them to the path, so I left the boys to water them and walked the last mile round the lake to the rest house.

This was a single-storeyed, white building comprising a dining-room, kitchen, verandah, and four minute bedrooms. The accommodation was very simple; there was, of course, no bath or sanitation and no glass in the windows. There was, however, a most delightfully amiable young Greek in charge of it, who got me a meal and talked incessantly in very obscure English. It was now about three o'clock. Seeing that I was tired, he said he would make me a cocktail. He took a large glass and poured into it, whisky, crème de menthe, and Fernet Branca, and filled up with soda-water. He made himself a glass of the same mixture, clinked glasses, and said, 'Cheerioh, damned sorry no ice.' As a matter of fact, it was surprisingly refreshing. After luncheon I went to my room and slept until late in the evening.

We dined together on tinned spaghetti and exceedingly tough fried chicken. He prattled on about his home in Alexandria and his sister who was taking a secretarial course and his rich uncle who lived at Dirre-Dowa and had set him up in the inn. I asked what the uncle did, and he said he had a 'monopole'; this seemed to be a perfectly adequate description of almost all commercial ventures in Abyssinia. I could not gather what he monopolised; whatever it was seemed extremely profitable and involved frequent excursions to Aden. The nephew hoped to succeed to the business on his uncle's retirement.

While we were dining, two heavily armed soldiers appeared with a message for my host. He seemed mildly put out by their arrival, explaining with great simplicity that he was involved in an affair with an elderly Abyssinian lady of high birth; she was not very attractive, but what choice had he in a remote place like this? She was generous, but very exacting. Only that afternoon he had been with her and here were her retainers come to fetch him again. He gave them each a cigarette and told them to wait. When they had finished smoking, they returned; he offered them more cigarettes, but they refused; apparently their mistress was impatient; the young man shrugged and, excusing himself with the phrase (typical of his diction) 'You won't allow me, won't you?' went away with them into the darkness. I returned to my bed and slept.

Next morning we rode into Harar. The way was full of traffic, caravans of camels, mules and asses, horsemen, and teams of women bent double under prodigious loads of wood. There were no carts of any kind; indeed, I think that they are quite unknown in Abyssinia, and that the railway engine was the first wheeled vehicle to appear there. After three hours' gentle ride we came in sight of the town. Approached from Haramaya it presents a quite different aspect from the drawing in Burton's *First Steps in Africa*; there it appears as he saw it coming from the Somali coast, perched on a commanding hill; we found it lying below us, an irregular brown patch at the foot of the hills. In the distance rose the flat-topped mountain which the Abyssinians have chosen for their refuge in the event of the country rising against them; there is a lake of fresh water at the summit, and a naturally fortified camp which they hope to hold against the Galla until relief arrives from their own highlands. No one may visit the place without a permit from the local dedejmatch.

A few buildings – the British consulate, Lej Yasu's deserted palace, a Capuchin leper settlement, a church, and the villas of one or two Indian merchants – have spread beyond the walls; outside the main gate a few women squatting beside little heaps of grain and peppers constituted a market; there was a temporary and rather unstable arch of triumph presented to the town by the firm of Mohammedali in honour of the coronation. A guard was posted at the gate; there was also an octroi, where we had to leave the luggage until the officer should return from his luncheon some hours later.

As in most mediæval towns, there was no direct street in

Harar leading from the gates to the central square. A very narrow lane ran, under the walls, round numerous corners before it turned inwards and broadened into the main street. On either side of this passage stood ruined houses, desolate heaps of stone and rubble, some of them empty, others patched up with tin to accommodate goats or poultry. The town, like the numerous lepers who inhabit it, seemed to be dying at its extremities; the interior, however, was full of vitality and animation.

There are two inns in Harar, boasting the names of Leon d'Or and Bellevue; both universally condemned as unsuitable for European habitation. Any doubt I might have had about which to patronise was dissolved, as soon as we turned into the main street, by a stout little man in a black skull-cap, who threw himself at my bridle and led me to the Leon d'Or. During my brief visit I became genuinely attached to this man. He was an Armenian of rare character, named Bergebedgian; he spoke a queer kind of French with remarkable volubility, and I found great delight in all his opinions; I do not think I have ever met a more tolerant man; he had no prejudice or scruples of race, creed, or morals of any kind whatever; there were in his mind none of those opaque patches of inconsidered principles, it was a single translucent pool of placid doubt; whatever splashes of precept had disturbed its surface from time to time had left no ripple; reflections flitted to and fro and left it unchanged.

Unfortunately his hotel was less admirable. Most of his business was done in the bar, where he sold great quantities of colourless and highly inflammatory spirit distilled by a fellow countryman of his and labelled, capriciously, 'Very Olde Scotts Whisky', 'Fine Champayne', or 'Hollands Gin' as the taste of his clients dictated. Next to the bar was a little dining-room where two or three regular customers (also fellow countrymen) took their greasy and pungent meals. The bedrooms were built round a little courtyard, where some pathetic survivals of a garden were discernible amid the heaps of kitchen refuse with which it was littered. This building had formerly been the town house of an Abyssinian official. It was rarely that anyone came to stay; usually not more than one in any three weeks, he said; but, as it happened, there was a second guest at that moment, a French clerk on business from the Banque d'Indo-Chine at Djibouti. I lunched with this young man, who was a punctilious, mannerly person; the hot wind had chapped his lips so that he was unable to smile – an affliction which made him seem a little menacing in light conversation. It was he who first put into my head the deplorable notion of returning to Europe across the Congo by the west coast. The proprietor waited on us in person, and made it hard to escape the forbidding dishes: we both felt moderately ill after every meal.

That afternoon I went for a walk round the town and saw that a large part of it was in decay. The most prominent buildings were the modern Government House, the French hospital, Mohammedali's offices, a Capuchin mission cathedral, and an ancient mosque with two whitewashed minarets; the rest of the place was made up of a bunch of small shops, a few Armenian, Greek, and Indian stores, single-roomed dwelling-houses, mostly standing back behind grubby little yards, and numerous tedj houses, combined brothels and public houses which advertise themselves with a red cross over the door – a traditional sign which caused some misunderstanding when the Swedish medical mission first established itself in the country.

The appearance of the buildings and the people was wholly foreign to Abyssinia; a difference which was emphasised on this particular afternoon by the fact that all the Abyssinians were indoors at a party at Government House, so that the streets were peopled almost exclusively by turbaned Harari. The beauty of the women was dazzling – far exceeding anything I had expected. The native women I had seen at Addis Ababa had been far from attractive; their faces had been plump and smug, their hair unbecomingly heaped up in a black, fuzzy mass, glittering with melted butter, their figures swollen grotesquely with a surfeit of petticoats. The women of Harar are slender and very upright; they carry themselves with all the grace of the Somalis, but, instead of their monkey-like faces and sooty complexions, they had golden brown skins and features of the utmost fineness.

Moreover, there was a delicacy about their clothes and ornaments which the Somalis entirely lacked; their hair was plaited
into innumerable tight little ropes and covered with bright
silk shawls; they wore long trousers and silk shawls wound
under their arms, leaving their shoulders bare. Most of them
had bright gold ornaments. Burton admits their beauty, but
condemns their voices as harsh and outstandingly displeas-
ing. I cannot conceive what prompted this statement; indeed,
compared with those of Arab women, they seemed soft and
sweet. (No sound made by mankind is quite so painful as
the voices of two Arab women at variance.) An alliance might
be formed with any of these exquisite people, the Armenian
informed me later, for four thalers a month and board. That
it was possible that the parents might expect more in the
case of a foreigner. This sum, however, covered the girl's
services in the house, so that it was a perfectly sound investment if I intended making a stay of any length in the town.
I explained that I was only there for three days. In that case,
he said, it was obviously more convenient to confine myself
to married women. There were certain preliminary formal-
ities to be gone through with an unmarried girl which cost
time and money.[1]

I visited the leper settlement; a little collection of *tukals*

---

1. The Harari, in common with the Somalis and most of the Gallas,
practise infibulation.

outside the walls, in the charge of a French priest. Four or five sleep in each hut, an arrangement which the old priest explained in what seems to me a very terrible phrase, 'You understand, monsieur, that it takes several lepers to make one man.'

I went to the cathedral and there met the Bishop of Harar, the famous Monsignor Jerome, of whom I had heard many reports in Addis Ababa. He has been in the country for forty-eight years, suffering, at first, every kind of discouragement and persecution, and attaining, towards the middle of his career, a position of great influence at Court. He acted as Tafari's tutor, and many people attributed to him, often in harsh terms, the emperor's outstanding skill as a political tactician. Lately, as his pupil's ambitions have become real-ised, the bishop's advice has been less devotedly canvassed. Indeed, it is doubtful whether it would still be of great value, for he is a very old man now and his mind is losing some-thing of its former grasp of public affairs.

It is his practice to greet all visitors to his church, but I did not know this at the time and was greatly startled when he suddenly swooped in upon me. He was tall and emaci-ated, like an El Greco saint, with very long white hair and beard, great roving eyes, and a nervous, almost ecstatic smile; he advanced at a kind of shuffling jog-trot, fluttering his hands and uttering little moans. After we had been round the church, which was shabby and unremarkable enough, he invited me into his divan to talk. I steered the conversation as delicately as I could from church expenses to Arthur Rimbaud. At first we were at cross purposes, because the bishop, being a little deaf, mistook my '*poète*' for '*prêtre*', and inflexibly maintained that no Father Rimbaud had ever, to his knowledge, ministered in Abyssinia. Later this difficulty was cleared up, and the bishop, turning the name over in his mind, remembered that he had, in fact, known Rimbaud quite well; a young man with a beard, who was in some trouble with his leg; a very serious man who did not go out much; he was always worried about business; not a good Catholic, though he had died at peace with the Church, the bishop understood, at Marseille. He used to live with a native woman in a little house, now demolished, in the square; he had no children; probably the woman was still alive; she was not a native of Harar, and after Rimbaud's death she had gone back to her own people in Tigre . . . a very, very serious young man, the bishop repeated. He seemed to find this epithet the most satisfactory – very serious and sad.

It was rather a disappointing interview. All the way to Harar I had nurtured the hope of finding something new about Rimbaud, perhaps even to encounter a half-caste son keeping a shop in some back street. The only significant thing I learned from the bishop was that, living in Harar, surrounded by so many radiant women, he should have chosen a mate from the stolid people of Tigre – a gross and perverse preference.

That evening, at about six o'clock, Mr Bergebedgian suggested that we might go to the Abyssinian party which had
now finished luncheon and was settling down to an evening's music at Government House. He himself was an
indispensable guest, as he had promised the loan of an Aladdin lamp, without which they would be left in complete
darkness. Accordingly, we set out and were received with
great warmth by the acting governor. A considerable sum had
apparently been granted to the municipality to be spent on
rejoicings for the coronation, an object which was rightly
interpreted as meaning a series of parties. They had been
going on for a fortnight and would continue until the dedejmatch returned from the capital. As a symbol of the origin
of the feast, a kind of altar had been built, at one end of the
room, on which stood a large photograph of Tafari surrounded by flowers. About fifty Abyssinians in white *chammas*
sat round on the floor, already fairly drunk. Green chairs of
the kind one finds in public parks were set for us at a velvet-
covered round table. The acting governor sat with us and
poured out extravagant glasses of whisky. Slaves trotted about
among the other guests, distributing bottles of German beer.
With the appearance of our lamp the entertainment began.
An orchestra emerged, furnished with three single-stringed
fiddles. The singer was an Abyssinian woman of startling girth.
She sang in a harsh voice, panting for breath between each
line. It was an immensely long ballad of patriotic sentiment.

The name Haile Selassie recurred with great regularity. No one paid any more attention than they would have at a musical party in Europe, but she sang on cheerfully, through the buzz of conversation, with an expression of settled amiability. When a gate-crasher was detected and expelled with some disorder, she merely turned round and watched the proceedings, still singing lustily. At the end of her song she was given some beer and many friendly smacks on the behind. The whisky was reserved for us and for a few favoured guests; the host singled these out, called for their glasses, and poured it into their beer from the bottle on the table.

The second song was a great deal longer than the first; it was of the kind, popular in European cabarets, which introduces references to members of the audience. Each name was greeted with cheers and a good deal of boisterous back-smacking. The host asked our names and repeated them in her ear, but they came out so distorted, if they came out at all, as to be wholly unrecognisable. After about two hours, Mr Bergebedgian said he must return to the inn and see to the dinner. This was the signal for a general movement; three or four notables were invited to the table, wine-glasses produced, a dish of sponge fingers, and finally a bottle of champagne. We drank each other's health, making graceful unintelligible little speeches in our own languages. Then, after much handshaking, we returned to the inn, leaving our Aladdin lamp at the party.

After a profoundly indigestible dinner, Mr Bergebedgian joined us – the unsmiling clerk and myself – in a glass of a disturbing liqueur labelled 'Koniak'. Presently he said, would we like to go to another party? There was a wedding in the town. We said we should like to go very much. This time our expedition was attended with grave precautions. First, Mr Bergebedgian buckled on bandoleer and revolver-holster; then he went to the cash-desk and produced a heavy automatic pistol, charged the magazine, and tucked it into place; then he reached under the bar and drew out four or five wooden clubs, which he dealt out to his servants; the bank-clerk showed a revolver, I my sword-stick; he nodded approval. It was all very much like Rat's preparation for the attack on Toad Hall. Then he barred up the house, a process involving innumerable bolts and padlocks. At last, attended by three servants with staves and a storm lantern, we set out. Things were safer at Harar than they used to be, he explained, but it was wiser to take no risks. As we emerged into the street, a hyena flashed red eyes at us and scuttled off. I do not know how hyenas have got their reputation for laughing. Abyssinia is full of them; they come into the towns at night scavenging and performing the less valuable service of nosing up corpses in the cemeteries; they used to bay all round the hotel at Addis Ababa, and the next night, which I spent in a tent in the Plowmans' garden, was disturbed by a small pack of them crunching bones within a few yards of my bed, but not once did I hear anything approaching a laugh.

The streets were pitch black – not a lighted window showed anywhere – and except for hyenas, dogs, and cats fighting over the refuse, totally deserted. Our way led down a narrow passage, between high, crumbling walls, which was sometimes graded in steps and sometimes sloped steeply inwards to a dry gutter. Our first stop was at the house of a Greek grocer. We beat on the shutters, behind which a crack of light was immediately extinguished. Mr Bergebedgian called his name, and presently a little peep opened and a pair of eyes appeared. Some civilities were exchanged, and then, after much drawing of bolts, we were admitted. The grocer offered us 'koniak' and cigarettes. Mr Bergebedgian explained that we wanted him to accompany us to the party. He refused, explaining that he had to make up his books. Mr Bergebedgian, accordingly, borrowed some small silver (a loan which, I observed, was duly noted in the accounts) and we took our leave. More black, empty alleys. Suddenly a policeman rocketed up from the gutter where he had been taking a rest, and challenged us with some ferocity. Mr Bergebedgian replied with a mock flourish of his revolver; some light exchange of chaff and back-chat followed, in the course of which the policeman decided to join the party. After a few minutes we found another policeman, huddled in his blanket on the counter of a deserted greengrocer's stall; they shook him awake and brought him along with us. At last, we reached a small courtyard, beyond which, from a lighted door, came the sound of singing.

No doubt we looked rather a formidable gang as we stalked in bristling with weapons, but it was probably the sight of the two policemen which caused most alarm. Anyway, whatever the reason, wild panic followed our entry. There was only one door, through which we had come, and a stream of Harari girls dashed past us, jostling, stumbling, and squealing; others cowered away under their shawls or attempted to climb the steps which led to a little loft. Mr Bergebedgian repeatedly explained our pacific intentions, but it was some time before confidence was restored. Then a young man appeared with chairs for us and the dance was resumed.

The house consisted of a single room with a gallery full of coffee sacks at one end approached by a ladder. This corner was the kitchen. A large stove, built of clay and rubble, stood under the ladder, and two or three earthenware jars and pots lay on and around it. Opposite the door the floor was raised in a carpeted dais which extended in a narrow ledge down the adjoining wall. It was here that our chairs were set. The few men of the party lounged round the door; the girls squatted together on the dais; the dance took place in the well of the floor to the music of the girls, singing, and the beating of hand drums. It was a pretty scene, lit by a single oil-lamp; the walls were decorated with coloured wicker-work plates; a brazier of charcoal and incense stood in one corner; a wicker dish of sweets was passed from one delicate henna-stained hand to another among the girls on the dais.

The dance was of the simplest kind. One girl and two men stood opposite each other; the girl wore a shawl on her head and the men held their *chammas* over the lower part of their faces. They shuffled up to each other and shuffled back; after several repetitions of this movement they crossed over, revolving as they passed each other, and repeated the figure from opposite sides. As the girl came to our end, Mr Bergebedgian pulled her shawl off. 'Look,' he said, 'hasn't she got nice hair?' She recovered it crossly and Mr Bergebedgian began teasing her, twitching it back every time she passed. But he was a soft-hearted fellow and he desisted as soon as he realised he was causing genuine distress.

This was the bride's house that we were in; a second party was in progress in another part of the town at the home of the bridegroom. We went to visit it and found it precisely similar in character, but very much larger and more splendid. Clearly the girl had made a good match. These parties are kept up every night for a week before the wedding; the bride's friends and relations in her home, the bridegroom's in his. They do not mix until the actual wedding-day. For some reason which I could not fathom they had lately come under ban of the law; hence the consternation at our arrival.

We stayed for about an hour and then returned to our hotel. The policemen came in with us and hung about until they were given a tumblerful each of neat spirit. Sleep was difficult that night, for the pillows were hard as boards, and through the windows, devoid of glass and shutters, came the incessant barking of dogs and hyenas and the occasional wailing horns of the town guard.

Next morning the bank-clerk rode away and Mr Bergebedgian took me for a walk in the town. He was a remarkable guide. We went into the shops of all his friends and drank delicious coffee and smoked cigarettes; he seemed to have small financial transactions with all of them, paying out a thaler here, receiving another there. We went into the law-courts, where we saw a magistrate trying a case about real property; for some reason both litigants and all the witnesses were in chains; the plaintiff was a Galla who pleaded his own cause through an interpreter. He became so eager about his wrongs that the interpreter was unable to keep up with him, and after repeated admonishments left him to finish his own case in his own tongue. Behind the court was a lion in a wooden case so small that he could barely move in it, so foul that the air of the whole yard was insupportable. We saw the great hall used for the raw-beef banquets. A group of slave-boys were being instructed in squad drill by an older boy with a stick. The commands were recognisably of English origin – presumably imported by some old soldier from the

KAR. We went into the prison, a place of frightful filth, only comparable to the lion's cage. Mr Bergebedgian, in whose character there was a marked strain of timidity, was very reluctant to enter, saying that three or four deaths occurred there every week from typhus; a flea from one of the prisoners would kill us both. That evening in my bath I found myself covered with flea-bites, and remembered this information with some apprehension. I was not really at ease in my mind until the time was over for the disease to show itself. The cells stood round a small yard; three or four men were tethered to the wall of each cell, with chains just long enough to allow of their crawling into the open. Those who were fed by their families never left the buildings; the others were allowed to earn their keep by working in gangs on the roads. The lot of the more neglected seemed by far preferable. Most of the prisoners were there for debt, often for quite trifling sums; they remained there until they paid or, more probably, died. There were no less than three prisons in Harar. My servant got locked up one day for a breach of the sanitary regulations and I had to pay five dollars to get him out. He remarked, with some justice, how could one tell that there were any sanitary regulations in Harar? In his opinion, it was a put-up job because he was a stranger.

We went into the two or three *tedj* houses. At this stage of the morning they were fairly empty, some had no customers at all, in others a few dissipated men, who had slept the night there, squatted holding their heads, quarrelling with the women about the reckoning; at only one did we find any gaiety, where a party just arrived from the country were starting to get drunk; each sat beside a decanter of cloudy *tedj*, one of them was playing a kind of banjo. The women were, without exception, grossly ugly. Mr Bergebedgian drew back a sleeve and exhibited a sore on the shoulder of one of them. 'A dirty lot,' he said, giving her an affectionate pat and a half-piastre bit.

We went through the bazaar, Mr Bergebedgian disparaging all the goods in the friendliest way possible, and I bought some silver bangles which he obtained for me at a negligible fraction of their original price. We went into several private houses, where Mr Bergebedgian examined and exhibited everything, pulling clothes out of the chests, bringing down bags of spice from the shelves, opening the oven and tasting the food, pinching the girls, and giving half-piastre pieces to the children. We went into a workshop where three or four girls of dazzling beauty were at work making tables and trays of fine, brilliantly patterned basket-work. Everywhere he went he seemed to be welcome; everywhere he not only adapted, but completely transformed, his manners to the environment. When I came to consider the question I was surprised to realise that the two most accomplished men I met during the six months I was abroad, the chauffeur who took us to Debra Lebanos and Mr Bergebedgian, should both have been Armenians. A race of rare competence and the most delicate sensitivity. They seem to me the only genuine 'men of the world'. I suppose everyone at times likes to picture himself as such a person. Sometimes, when I find that elusive ideal looming too attractively, when I envy among my friends this one's adaptability to diverse company, this one's cosmopolitan experience, this one's impenetrable armour against sentimentality and humbug, that one's freedom from conventional prejudices, this one's astute ordering of his finances and nicely calculated hospitality, and realise that, whatever happens to me and however I deplore it, I shall never in actual fact become a 'hardboiled man of the world' of the kind I read about in the novels I sometimes obtain at bookstalls for short railway journeys; that I shall always be ill at ease with nine out of every ten people I meet; that I shall always find something startling and rather abhorrent in the things most other people think worth doing, and something puzzling in their standards of importance; that I shall probably be increasingly, rather than decreasingly, vulnerable to the inevitable minor disasters and injustices of life – then I comfort myself a little by thinking that, perhaps, if I were an Armenian I should find things easier.

After luncheon, a very discomforting meal, I assembled my staff and rode out to the consulate on the hillside opposite, where the Plowmans had returned that morning. It was a house of some age, standing in a large garden, and here I spent three restful days.

The consul and I went to another celebration at Government House, an afternoon party for the six or seven European residents — the French doctor, two priests, two Swedish school teachers and the Italian consul. We sat round a table in the same room and drank champagne and ate sponge fingers. I visited Mr Bergebedgian once or twice and saw the religious dances at the church for the feast of St Michael. Then I resumed my travels. I had intended to stay there for only two nights, having an idea that my train to Djibouti left Dirre-Dowa on Saturday evening. I was assured, however, that it was not until Sunday, so I stayed on until Saturday afternoon, resting that night at Haramaya and reaching the station after a tiring but uneventful ride at midday on Sunday.

There I learned that my train had left on the previous evening. The next started on Tuesday morning and arrived at Djibouti about two hours after the advertised time of the *Général Voyron*'s sailing. I telegraphed to the Messageries' agent, begging him to delay the ship, and resigned myself to a tedious week-end.

FIRST NIGHTMARE

When we have been home from abroad for a week or two, and time after time, in answer to our friends' polite inquiries, we have retold our experiences, letting phrase engender phrase, until we have made quite a good story of it all; when the unusual people we encountered have, in retrospect, become fabulous and fantastic, and all the checks and uncertainties of travel have become very serious dangers; when the minor annoyances assume heroic proportions and have become, at the luncheon-table, barely endurable privations; even before that, when in the later stages of our journey we reread in our diaries the somewhat bald chronicle of the preceding months – how very little attention do we pay, among all these false frights and bogies, to the stark horrors of boredom.

It seems to me that not nearly enough has been said about this aspect of travel. No one can have any conception of what boredom really means until he has been to the tropics. The boredom of civilised life is trivial and terminable, a puny thing to be strangled between finger and thumb. The blackest things in European social life – rich women talking about their poverty, poor women talking about their wealth, week-end parties of Cambridge æsthetes or lecturers from the London School of Economics, rival Byzantinists at variance, actresses off the stage, psychologists explaining one's own books to one, Americans explaining how much they have drunk lately, houseflies at early morning in the South of France, amateur novelists talking about royalties and reviews, amateur journalists, quarrelling lovers, mystical atheists, raconteurs, dogs, Jews conversant with the group movements of Montparnasse, people who try to look inscrutable, the very terrors, indeed, which drive one to refuge in the still-remote regions of the earth, are mere pansies and pimpernels to the rank flowers which flame grossly in those dark and steaming sanctuaries.

I am constitutionally a martyr to boredom, but never in Europe have I been so desperately and degradingly bored as I was during the next four days; they were as black and time-less as Damnation; a handful of fine ashes thrown into the eyes, a blanket over the face, a mass of soft clay knee deep. My diary reminds me of my suffering in those very words, but the emotion which prompted them seems remote. I know a woman who is always having babies; every time she resolves that that one shall be the last. But, every time, she forgets her resolution, and it is only when her labour begins that she cries to midwife and husband, 'Stop, stop; I've just remembered what it is like. I refuse to have another.' But it is then too late. So the human race goes on. Just in this way, it seems to me, the activity of our ant-hill is preserved by a merciful process of oblivion. 'Never again,' I say on the steps of the house, 'never again will I lunch with that woman.' 'Never again,' I say in the railway carriage, 'will I go and stay with those people.' And yet a week or two later the next invitation finds me eagerly accepting. 'Stop,' I cry inwardly, as I take my hostess's claw-like hand. 'Stop, stop,' I cry in my tepid bath; 'I have just remembered what it is like. I refuse to have another.' But it is too late.

From time to time I meet people who say they are never bored; they are of two kinds; both, for the most part, liars. Some are equally entranced by almost all observable objects, a straggle of blossom on a whitewashed wall, chimneys against the sky, two dogs on a muck heap, an old man with a barrow . . . Precepts of my house master, a very indolent clergyman, rise before me . . . 'only a dull boy is ever dull' . . . 'the world is so full of a number of things' . . .

Others find consolation in their own minds. Whenever they are confronted with a dreary prospect, they tell me, they just slip away from the barren, objective world into the green pastures and ivory palaces of imagination. Perhaps, by a kind of arrested development, some of them really have retained this happy faculty of childhood, but as a rule I find that both these boasts boil down to a simple form of pessimism – the refusal to recognise that any particular human activity can be of greater value than any other one.

Has anyone ever compiled an anthology of bored verse? It would make a pretty Christmas book with Richard Sickert's 'Ennui' as Frontispiece. Shakespeare and the Bible are full of passages that might be quoted; then there is Mr Herbert's housemaid's song from *Riverside Nights*, and the wartime 'Nobody knows how bored we are, and nobody seems to care'. There might be an appendix of suicides' letters which appear constantly in the daily Press and are too soon forgotten, confessions of faith by men in early middle age who say: '*I am fed up and have resolved to end it all. It just goes on and on. Yesterday the clock broke and there is four shillings owing for the milk. Tell Ruby the key of the coal-cellar is under the hat upstairs. There is not any coal. I have not been a bad man, but I couldn't stand it. Give Aunt Loo my love; she was always one of the best. If the milkman says it's more, it is only four shillings.*'

I wish I could write an account worthy of inclusion in that anthology of the four days between Harar and Aden, but the truth is that they have become vague and insignificant. The suffering was genuine enough, but like a mother emerging from twilight sleep, I am left with only the vague impression that nothing much happened.

Nothing much happened. After luncheon I paid off my mules, the guide, the porter, and the old man who had, by sheer persistence at some indefined moment during the journey, become recognised as a legitimate member of my suite.

Then I sat in Mr Bollolakos' hotel.

Outside in the empty streets the white dust lay radiant and miasmic. Inside there was shade. The bar was locked; the servants were all asleep. The courtyard was unendurable. There was only one place to sit – a small square parlour with cement floor and whitewashed walls; in the centre a table with a plush cloth over it, against the walls a rickety wicker couch and two iron rocking-chairs. I had nothing to read except the first volume of a pocket edition of Pope. There are moments when one does not want to read Pope; when one requires something bulky and informative. There was no bookshop or newsagent in the town. Most hotels, however simple, harbour some reading-matter of some sort or other: brochures of advertisement, magazines or novels left by previous visitors, a few postcards on a rack . . . At Mr Bollolakos' there was nothing.

For an hour or two I sat in the rocking-chair reading Pope's juvenile poems.

Most of the time I thought about how awful the next day would be.

In my bedroom were three more volumes of Pope and some writing-paper.

But I should have to cross the courtyard to get to my bedroom.

Presently I got more uninterested in Pope's juvenile poems and decided to cross the courtyard. The three volumes of Pope were somewhere at the bottom of my bag; but I found the writing-paper quite easily; also a minute French dictionary I had forgotten about.

I sat for an hour or so and read the French dictionary, rocking the iron chair in the parlour. 'Bourrasque, f., squall; fit. Bourre, f., wadding; trash. Bourreau, m., executioner.' . . .

Presently I drew the table up to the wicker couch, rolled back the plush covering, and wrote a great many letters of Christmas greetings to everyone in England whose address I could remember. I said that it was lovely in Abyssinia; that I pitied them in the fogs and monotony of London; that I longed to see them again and hear all their scandal; that I should be home early in the New Year; that I had bought them presents of shocking Abyssinian painting, which I would deliver on my return to England – every word was a lie.

At sunset the servants woke up; the bar was opened; tables were brought out into the courtyard and laid for dinner; Mr and Mrs Hall and the Cypriot bank-manager arrived. I told them that I had no books, and they compassionately lent me some copies of John o' London's Weekly. Mr Hall was most amiable. He led me back to his house after dinner and showed me some pastel drawings he had made of Ethiopian sunsets, and a coloured photograph of the Prince of Wales which stood on a draped easel in a corner of the drawing-room.

His invitation for the coronation had arrived by yesterday's mail; intrigue in high places had delayed it, he said; there were many members of the commercial community who were jealous of his wife's jewellery; and he nodded significantly to the fine brooch commemorating the opening of Epping Forest to the public.

That night, under my mosquito curtain, I read three issues of *John o' London's Weekly* straight through, word for word, from cover to cover.

Next morning after breakfast I read the fourth. Then I went up to the bank and dragged out the cashing of a small cheque to the utmost limits of politeness; I sent a letter of introduction to the famous M. de Montfried, but learned that he was in Europe. It was still early in the day. I took a dose of sleeping-draught and went to bed again.

That evening the train from Hawash arrived, bringing the old gentleman with whom I had travelled to Addis Ababa and one of the ladies who had been staying at the legation. He was on his way to visit the Plowmans at Harar; she was going to the coast and then to Europe. The latest news from Addis was that everyone felt very tired.

Early next morning the train left for Djibouti. There was none of the formality or facility that had characterised our arrival. Half an hour after the train was due to start, the lady from the legation and I were turned out of the carriages which she had occupied on the previous two days, to make room for the servants of an Abyssinian princess who was running down to the coast for a little shopping. These men were very drunk and employed their time in throwing beer-bottles into the desert from the observation platform. With every mile of the journey the heat and humidity became worse; the country on either side of the line was unrelieved emptiness; we rattled and jolted very slowly along the narrow track, increasing by another hour and a half the delay which the royal party had caused, while the young lady from the legation entertained me with censorious comments on the two or three English and Irish acquaintances whom we found in common.

There was one moment of excitement when, towards sundown, we came in sight of the sea and saw that the *Général Voyron* was still there. She lay far out in the harbour, with steam up, presumably waiting for the train. The line into Djibouti turns and twists among great boulders and dry watercourses, so that sometimes we lost sight of her for ten minutes at a time; with every reappearance she seemed further away. Presently it became clear that she had, in fact, already sailed.

I discussed the question with the Messageries agent, but he was unpenitent. I had said in my telegram that I was coming at five-thirty; he had kept the ship back until six; I had arrived at seven; it was not his affair that the train was late; sometimes on that line trains were several days late. This

attitude is described, by those who like it, as Latin logic. It
is true that Armenians do not see things in the same terms.

We went to the Hôtel des Arcades. Madame's geniality
seemed less comforting than it had done on my first arrival.
We visited the British vice-consul to ask about ships and
learned that there was one to Europe on Thursday and a
small boat to Aden on Saturday; the next Messageries ship to
Zanzibar left in a fortnight; he said that there had been several little earthquakes during the last month and showed us
a large fissure in the wall of his office.

I returned to the hotel in low spirits. From any point of
view the prospect seemed unsatisfactory. The primary need
seemed to be immediate escape from Djibouti. I had practically made up my mind to return to Europe when Madame
at the hotel came to my rescue. There was an Italian boat
leaving for Aden next day; the Messageries ship from Zanzibar would pick me up there. We dined on the pavement and
I went to bed more hopefully.

Next day was the most deadly of all. I was awakened at
dawn with information that the Italian boat was in, and was
leaving in an hour. I dressed in haste, fastened my luggage,
and hurried downstairs. Madame greeted me in a pink peignoir.
The boy had made a mistake. There was no boat in.

As soon as it was open I went to the Italian shipping office
and bought my ticket. Their ship was due at any time, and
would leave within an hour or two of her arrival. She was

called the Somalia. They would ring me up at the hotel as soon as she was sighted. I sat about the hotel all day waiting for their message; it was impossible to go far away. We visited the chief store of the town and bought some books; the Abyssinian princess was there in a heavy green veil, bargaining over a pseudo-Chinese dinner-gong of atrocious construction. At dinner-time the shipping company rang up to say that the Somalia was not expected until next morning. Later that evening I discovered that there were three American cinema-men staying at the other hotel; their company was very pleased with them for the pictures they had made of the coronation, and they were pleased with themselves. We went for an exquisitely dismal jaunt together in the native town.

Next day was pretty bad. I was again called at dawn with the news that the Somalia was in and would sail directly. This time the information was partially correct. I paid, in my haste without questioning it, an hotel bill of staggering size, and hurried down to the sea. The Somalia was there all right, a clean little coastal steamer with accommodation for half a dozen passengers. When I had embarked I learned that she was not sailing until six that evening. I had not the spirit to return to the shore; I watched the liner for Europe arrive, take up the lady from the legation, and steam away. All that day I sat on a swivel chair in the saloon, reading one of the books I had purchased at the store – a singularly ill-informed account of Abyssinia, translated from the English.

Eventually, rather after six o'clock, we sailed, and crossed in fine weather to Aden. There were five of us at dinner that night – the captain, a French clerk, and an Italian official and his wife on their way to Mogadishu. We had nothing much to say to each other. The Italian official made some jokes about sea-sickness; the French clerk gave me some figures, whose significance I have now forgotten, about the coffee trade at Hodeida; the captain was gallant in Italian to the official's wife.

Next morning we arrived at Aden. That was the end of four exceedingly painful days.

BRITISH EMPIRE

One

Pure mischance had brought me to Aden, and I expected to dislike it. I had, in fact, a fairly clear picture in my mind of what it would be like; a climate notoriously corrosive of all intellect and initiative; a landscape barren of any growing or living thing; a community, full of placid self-esteem, typical in part of Welwyn Garden City, in part of the Trocadero bar; conversation full of dreary technical shop among the men, and harsh little snobberies among the women. I contrasted it angrily with the glamour and rich beauty I expected to find at Zanzibar. How wrong I was.

How wrong I was, as things turned out, in all my preconceived notions about this journey. Zanzibar and the Congo, names pregnant with romantic suggestion, gave me nothing, while the places I found most full of interest were those I expected to detest – Kenya and Aden.

On first acquaintance, however, there was much about the settlement to justify my forebodings. It is, as every passenger down the Red Sea knows, an extinct volcano joined to the mainland by a flat and almost invisible neck of sand; not a tree or flower or blade of grass grows on it, the only vegetation is a meagre crop of colourless scrub which has broken out in patches among the cinders; there is no earth and no water, except what is dragged there in a ceaseless succession of camel-carts through the tunnelled road; the sanitation everywhere – in the hotels, the club, the mess, the private bungalows – is still that of a temporary camp. Architecture, except for a series of water-tanks of unknown age, does not exist. A haphazard jumble of bungalows has been spilt over the hillside, like the litter of picnic-parties after Bank Holiday. Opposite the quay a waste space has been faintly formalised and called a garden, and behind it stands a mean crescent, comprising shipping offices, two hotels, and a few shops peddling oriental trash in silk, brass, and ivory. The chief hotel is as expensive as Torr's at Nairobi; the food has only two flavours – tomato ketchup and Worcestershire sauce; the bathroom consists of a cubicle in which a tin can is suspended on a rope; there is a nozzle at the bottom of the can encrusted with stalactites of green slime; the bather stands on the slippery cement floor and pulls a string releasing a jet of water over his head and back; for a heavy extra charge it is possible, with due notice, to have the water warmed; the hall porter has marked criminal tendencies; the terrace is infested by money-changers. The only compensating luxury, a seedy, stuffed sea-animal, unmistakably male, which is kept in a chest and solemnly exhibited – on payment – as a mermaid. You would have to search a long time before finding many such hotels in the whole of England.

There are other superficial disadvantages about Aden, notably the division of the settlement into two towns. So far I have been speaking of the district known as Steamer Point; about three miles – an expensive taxi-drive – away lies Crater Town, the centre of such commerce as has survived. This was the original nucleus of the settlement. It is surrounded on three sides by cliffs, and on the fourth by what was once a harbour, now silted up and for a long time closed to all traffic. The original residency stands there, now a guesthouse for visiting Arab chiefs; there is also a large derelict barracks, partially demolished, and an Anglican church, built in Victorian Gothic, which was once the garrison chapel, and is still provided with its own chaplain, who reads services there Sunday after Sunday in absolute void. This man, earnest and infinitely kind, had lately arrived from Bombay; he rescued me from the hotel, and took me to stay with him for a few days in his large, ramshackle house on the Crater beach, known to taxi-drivers as 'Padre sahib's bungalow'. A few of the political officers still have quarters round the Crater, and there are a half-dozen or so British commercial agents and clerks: the rest of the population are mixed Asiatics, for the most part Indian, Arab, or Jew, with numerous Somalis and one or two Persians and Parsees, inhabiting a compact series of streets between the water and the hills.

Trade has been declining during recent years. Mokka coffee, which until lately was shipped through Aden, is now taken through Hodeida, while in her former important position as clearing house for skins she has been largely superseded by the small, French and Italian, Red Sea ports who now export directly to Europe. The inanition which descends on everyone in Aden is completing the dissolution; the business men still talk gloomily about the 'world slump', but it is clear to most honest observers that the chances of recovery are extremely small. In these circumstances there would probably be a general movement of Indian traders to East Africa; about sixty per cent of the population, however, consists of Arabic-speaking Mohammedans, who may be expected to survive the exodus. The problem of British policy will then arise: whether Crater Town will decay into an Arab village, crowded in the ruins of the infantry lines and the garrison chapel, like the Arab villages of North Africa among Roman fortifications, a 'picturesque bit' between an administrative post at Steamer Point and an air-base at Khormaksar, where liner passengers may take their Kodaks during an hour on shore, or whether it will be possible to make of it an Arab capital town, forming a centre for education, medical service, and arbitration for the tribes between the Hadramaut and the Yemen. Meanwhile, the town affords a remarkable variety of race and costume. Arabs are represented in every grade of civilisation, from courteous old gentlemen in Government service who wear gold-rimmed spectacles, silk turbans, and light frock coats and carry shabby umbrellas with highly decorated handles, to clusters of somewhat bemused Bedouin straight from the desert; these are, in appearance, very different from the noble savages of romance; their clothes consist of a strip of blanket round the waist, held up by a sash from which protrudes the hilt of a large dagger; their hair is straight, black, and greasy, lying on the back of the head in a loose bun and bound round the forehead with a piece of rag; they are of small stature and meagre muscular development; their faces are hairless or covered with a slight down, their expressions degenerate and slightly dotty, an impression which is accentuated by their loping, irregular gait.

The British political officer introduced me to a delightful Arab who acted as my interpreter and conducted me round Crater Town. He took me to his club, a large upper storey, where at the busy time of the commercial day we found the principal Arab citizens reclining on divans and chewing *khat*; later he took me to an Arab café where the lower class congregate; here, too, was the same decent respect for leisure; the patrons reclined round the walls in a gentle stupor, chewing *khat*. 'These simple people, too, have their little pleasures,' my companion remarked.

Later I received an invitation to tea from the president and committee of the club. This time the bundles of *khat* had been removed, and plates of sweet biscuits and dates and tins of cigarettes had taken their place. My friend and interpreter

was there, but the president – whose father was chief secretary to the Sultan of Lahej – spoke enough English to make
conversation very difficult.

I was introduced to about a dozen Arabs. We sat down in
two rows opposite each other. A servant brought in a tray of
tea and bottled lemonade. We talked about the distressing
conditions of local trade.

Everything would be all right and everyone would be
happy, said the Arabs, if only the bank would give longer and
larger overdrafts. I remarked that in England we are embarrassed in exactly that way too. They laughed politely.
Europeans, they said, could always get all the money they
wanted. Even Indians, a race renowned for dishonour and
instability, could get larger advances than the Arabs; how was
one to live unless one borrowed the money? They had heard
it said I was writing a book. Would I, in my book, persuade
the bank to lend them more money? I promised that I would
try. (Will any official of the Bank of India who reads this
book please let the Aden Arabs have more money?)

We talked about London. They told me that the Sultan of
Lahej had been there and had met the King-Emperor. We
talked about the King-Emperor and pretty Princess Eliza-
beth. I confess I am pretty bad at carrying on this kind of
conversation. There were several long pauses. One of them
was broken by the president suddenly saying, 'We all take
great sorrow at the loss of your R 101.'

I agreed that it had been a terrible disaster, and remarked that I knew one of the victims fairly well.

'We think it very sad,' said the president, 'that so many of your well-educated men should have been killed.'

That seemed to me a new aspect of the tragedy.

Conversation again languished, until one of the company, who had hitherto taken no part in the conversation, rose to his feet and, tucking up his shirt, exhibited the scars in his side caused by a recent operation for gall stone. This man was local correspondent to a London newspaper. He had lately, he told me, sent the foreign-news editor a complete genealogy of the Imam of Sana, compiled by himself with great labour. Did I know whether it had yet been printed, and, if not, could I put in a word for him in Fleet Street when I returned?

When the time came to leave, the president gave me an inscribed photograph of himself in Court uniform.

One evening there was a fair in Crater Town. There were stalls selling sweets and sherbet under naphtha flares, and tables with simple gambling-games. One of these was the simplest gambling-game I ever saw. The banker dealt five cards face downwards and the players placed a stake of an anna on one or other of them. When each card had found a backer – two players were not allowed to bet on the same card – they were turned up. The winning card was then paid even money and the banker pocketed three annas a time.

There was also a game played for tins of pineapple. Groups of men danced in circles between the stalls. The officer formerly in command of the Aden Levy told me the interesting fact that, when Arab troops are halted for refreshment during a route march, instead of lying down like Europeans, they make up little parties and dance. But I could not see anything specifically invigorating about the mild shuffling and clapping which they performed at this fair.

One unifying influence among the diverse cultures of the Crater was the Aden troop of Boy Scouts. It is true that Arabs cannot be induced to serve in the same patrol with Jews, but it is a remarkable enough spectacle to see the two races sitting amicably on opposite sides of a campfire, singing their songs in turn and occasionally joining each other in chorus. The scoutmaster, an English commercial agent, invited me to attend one of these meetings.

The quarters were a disused sergeants' mess and the former barrack square. My friend was chiefly responsible for the Arab patrol, the Jews having an independent organisation. As I approached, rather late, I saw the latter drilling in their own quarter of the parade ground – a squad of lengthy, sallow boys in very smart uniforms furnished with every possible accessory by the benefaction of a still-wealthy local merchant. The Arabs – with the exception of one resplendent little Persian, for 'Arab' in this connection was held to include all Gentiles, Somali, Arab, and Mohammedan Indians – were less luxuriously equipped. There were also far fewer of them. This was explained by the fact that two of the second-class scouts were just at that time celebrating their marriages.

Tests were in progress for the tenderfoot and other badges. The acquiring of various badges is a matter of primary concern in the Aden troop. Some of the children had their arms well covered with decorations. 'We generally let them pass after the third or fourth attempt,' the scoutmaster explained. 'It discourages them to fail too often.'

Two or three figures crouching against corners of masonry were engaged on lighting fires. This had to be done with two matches; they had been provided by their mothers with horrible messes of food in tin cans, which they intended to warm up and consume. I believe this qualified them for a cookery medal. 'Of course, it isn't like dealing with English boys,' said the scoutmaster; 'if one isn't pretty sharp they put paraffin on the sticks.'

The scoutmaster kept the matchbox, which was very quickly depleted. Breathless little creatures kept running up. 'Please, sahib, no burn. Please more matches.' Then we would walk across, scatter the assembled sticks and tinder, and watch them built up again. It was not a long process. A match was then struck, plunged into the centre of the little pile, and instantly extinguished. The second match followed. 'Please, sahib, no burn.' Then the business began again. Occasionally crows of delight would arise and we were hastily summoned to see a real conflagration. Now and then a sheet of flame would go up very suddenly, accompanied by a column of black smoke. 'Oil,' said the scoutmaster, and that fire would be disqualified.

Later a Somali boy presented himself for examination in scout law. He knew it all by heart perfectly. 'First scoot law a scoot's honour iss to be trust second scoot law . . .' et cetera, in one breath.

'Very good, Abdul. Now tell me what does "thrifty" mean?'

'Trifty min?'

'Yes, what do you mean, when you say a scout is thrifty?'

'I min a scoot hass no money.'

'Well, that's more or less right. What does "clean" mean?'

'Clin min?'

'You said just now a scout is clean in thought, word, and deed.'

'Yis, scoot iss clin.'

'Well, what do you mean by that?'

'I min tought, worden deed.'

'Yes, well, what do you *mean* by clean?'

Both parties in this dialogue seemed to be losing confidence in the other's intelligence.

'I min the tenth scoot law.'

A pause during which the boy stood first on one black leg, then on the other, gazing patiently into the sun.

'All right, Abdul. That'll do.'

'Pass, sahib?'

'Yes, yes.'

An enormous smile broke across his small face, and away he went capering across the parade ground, kicking up dust over the fire-makers and laughing with pleasure.

'Of course, it isn't quite like dealing with English boys,' said the scoutmaster again.

Presently the two bridegrooms arrived, identically dressed in gala clothes, brilliantly striped silk skirts, sashes, and turbans, little coats and ornamental daggers. They were cousins, about fourteen years of age. They had been married a week ago. Tonight they were going to see their brides for the first time. They were highly excited by their clothes, and anxious to show them to their fellow scouts and scoutmaster.

Meanwhile the Jews had made a huge bonfire on the beach. Both patrols assembled round it and a short concert was held. They sang local songs in their own languages. I asked what they meant, but the scoutmaster was not sure. From what I know of most Arabic songs, I expect that they were wholly incompatible with the tenth scout law.

When, on leaving, I thanked the scoutmaster for his entertainment he said, 'Did you really find it interesting?'

'Yes, indeed I did.'

'Well, then, perhaps you won't think it such cheek what I am going to ask. We thought of starting a patrol magazine. I wondered if you would write us a short story for it. Just some little thing, you know, to do with scouting in different parts of the world.'

I thought it simplest to agree, but I do not feel very guilty at not having kept that promise. After all, I was on a holiday.

I think that perhaps it was the predominance of bachelors at Steamer Point that made the English community there so unusually agreeable. On paper its composition was exactly what one would have assumed – Resident and ADC, some soldiers, a sailor, numerous airmen, India Office and colonial officials; just such a list as has made English colonial stations odious throughout the novel-reading world. It just happened that at Aden they were all peculiarly pleasant individuals. In fact, I think there is never anything essentially ludicrous about English officials abroad; it is the wives they marry that are so difficult; at Aden the centres of social intercourse were in the club and the messes, not at bunga-low 'sundowner'-parties. At Zanzibar the club was practic-ally empty from eight o'clock onwards – everyone was at home with his wife; at Aden the bar and the cardroom were full till midnight; there seemed to be no children in the town – at any rate, none were ever mentioned.

There was plenty of entertainment going on. During my brief visit – ten days only in Aden itself – there was a dance at the club, a ball at the residency, and a very convivial party given by the Sappers. There was also a cinematograph performance.

This is a singular feature of Aden life which occurs every Thursday on the roof of the Seamen's Institute. I went with the flight-commander, who had been in charge of the Air Mission at Addis. We dined first at the club with two of his officers. There were parties at the other tables, also bound for the cinema; there were also dinner-parties at many of the bungalows. People entertain for the cinema on Thursday nights as they do for dances in London. It is not a hundred yards from the club to the Seamen's Institute, but we drove there in two cars. Other parties were arriving; a few Somalis loitered round the entrance, watching the procession; the residency car, flag flying on the bonnet, was already there. Upstairs the roof was covered with deep wicker chairs. The front row was reserved for the Resident's party. The other seats were already two-thirds full. Everyone, of course, was in evening dress. It was a warm night, brilliant with stars (though here I may interpolate that there is a lot of nonsense talked about tropical constellations. South of Cairo I never saw a sky that nearly equalled the splendour of a northern clear night. As for the Southern Cross, which one so often sees described as 'a blazing jewel', it is as dim and formless as a handful of glow-worms).

The first film was a Pathé Gazette, showing the King leaving London for Bognor Regis twenty months previously, and an undated Grand National, presumably of about the same antiquity. A fine old slapstick comedy followed. I turned to remark to my host how much superior the early comedies were to those of the present day, but discovered, to my surprise, that he was fast asleep. I turned to my neighbour on the other side; his head had fallen back, his eyes were shut, his mouth wide open. His cigarette was gradually burning towards his fingers. I took it from him and put it out. The movement disturbed him. He shut his mouth and, without opening his eyes, said, 'Jolly good, isn't it?' Then his mouth fell open again. I looked about me and saw in the half-light reflected from the screen that with very few exceptions the entire audience were asleep. An abysmal British drama followed, called The Woman Who Did. It was about a feminist and an illegitimate child and a rich grandfather. The roof remained wrapped in sleep. It is one of the odd characteristics of the Aden climate that it is practically impossible to remain both immobile and conscious.

Later, 'God Save the King' was played on the piano. Everyone sprang alertly to attention and, completely vivacious once more, adjourned to the club for beer, oysters, and bridge.

Everyone was delightfully hospitable, and between meals I made a serious attempt to grasp some of the intricacies of Arabian politics; an attempt which more often than not took the form of my spreading a table with maps, reports, and note-books, and then falling into a gentle and prolonged stupor. I spent only one really strenuous afternoon. That was in taking 'a little walk over the rocks', with Mr Leblanc and his 'young men'.

Nothing in my earlier acquaintance with Mr Leblanc had given me any reason to suspect what I was letting myself in for when I accepted his invitation to join him in his little walk over the rocks. He was a general merchant, commercial agent, and shipowner of importance, the only European magnate in the settlement; they said of him that he thrived on risk and had made and lost more than one considerable fortune in his time. I met him dining at the residency, on my first evening in Aden. He talked of Abyssinia, where he had heavy business undertakings, with keen sarcasm; he expressed his contempt for the poetry of Rimbaud; he told me a great deal of very recent gossip about people in Europe; he produced, from the pocket of his white waistcoat, a Press-cutting about Miss Rebecca West's marriage; after dinner he played some very new gramophone records he had brought with him. To me, rubbed raw by those deadly four days at Dirre-Dowa and Djibouti, it was all particularly emollient and healing.

A day or two afterwards he invited me to dinner at his house in Crater. A smart car with a liveried Indian chauffeur came to fetch me. We dined on the roof; a delicious dinner; iced *vin rosé* – 'It is not a luxurious wine, but I am fond of it; it grows on a little estate of my own in the South of France' – and the finest Yemen coffee. With his very thin gold watch in his hand, Mr Leblanc predicted the rising of a star – I forget which. Punctual to the second, it appeared, green and malevolent, on the rim of the hills; cigars glowing under the night sky; from below the faint murmur of the native streets; all infinitely smooth and civilised.

At this party a new facet was revealed to me in the character of my host. Mr Leblanc the man of fashion I had seen. Here was Mr Leblanc the patriarch. The house where we sat was the top storey of his place of business; at the table sat his daughter, his secretary, and three of his 'young men'. The young men were his clerks, learning the business. One was French, the other two English lately down from Cambridge. They worked immensely hard – often, he told me, ten hours a day; often half-way through the night, when a ship was in. They were not encouraged to go to the club or to mix in the society of Steamer Point. They lived together in a house near Mr Leblanc's; they lived very well and were on terms of patriarchal intimacy with Mr Leblanc's family. 'If they go up to Steamer Point, they start drinking, playing cards, and spending money. Here, they work so hard that they cannot help saving. When they want a holiday they go round the coast visiting my agencies. They learn to know the country and the people; they travel in my ships; at the end of a year or two they have saved nearly all their money and they have learned business. For exercise we take little walks over the rocks together. Tennis and polo would cost them money. To walk in the hills is free. They get up out of the town into the cool air, the views are magnificent, the gentle exercise keeps them in condition for their work. It takes their minds, for a little, off business. You must come with us one day on one of our walks.'

I agreed readily. After the torpid atmosphere of Aden it would be delightful to take some gentle exercise in the cool air. And so it was arranged for the following Saturday afternoon. When I left, Mr Leblanc lent me a copy of Gide's *Voyage au Congo*.

Mr Leblanc the man of fashion I knew, and Mr Leblanc the patriarch. On Saturday I met Mr Leblanc the man of action, Mr Leblanc the gambler.

I was to lunch first with the young men at their 'mess' – as all communal *ménages* appear to be called in the East. I presented myself dressed as I had seen photographs of 'hikers', with shorts, open shirt, stout shoes, woollen stockings, a large walking-stick. We had an excellent luncheon, during which they told me how, one evening, they had climbed into the Parsees' death-house, and what a row there had been about it. Presently one of them said, 'Well, it's about time to change. We promised to be round at the old man's at half-past.'

'Change?'

'Well, it's just as you like, but I think you'll find those things rather hot. We usually wear nothing except shoes and shorts. We leave our shirts in the cars. They meet us on the bathing-beach. And if you've got any rubber-soled shoes I should wear them. Some of the rocks are pretty slippery.' Luckily I happened to have some rubber shoes. I went back to the chaplain's house, where I was then living, and changed. I was beginning to be slightly apprehensive.

Mr Leblanc looked magnificent. He wore newly creased white shorts, a silk openwork vest, and white *espadrilles* laced like a ballet dancer's round his ankles. He held a tuberose, sniffing it delicately. 'They call it an Aden lily sometimes,' he said. 'I can't think why.'

There was with him another stranger, a guest of Mr Leblanc's on a commercial embassy from an oil firm. 'I say, you know,' he confided in me, 'I think this is going to be a bit stiff. I'm scarcely in training for anything very energetic.'

We set out in the cars and drove to a dead end at the face of the cliffs near the ancient reservoirs. I thought we must have taken the wrong road, but everyone got out and began stripping off his shirt. The Leblanc party went hatless; the stranger and I retained our topis.

'I should leave those sticks in the car,' said Mr Leblanc.

'But shan't we find them useful?' (I still nursed memories of happy scrambles in the Wicklow hills.)

'You will find them a great nuisance,' said Mr Leblanc.

We did as we were advised.

Then the little walk started. Mr Leblanc led the way with light, springing steps. He went right up to the face of the cliff,

gaily but purposefully as Moses may have approached the
rocks from which he was about to strike water. There was a
little crack running like fork-lightning down the blank wall
of stone. Mr Leblanc stood below it, gave one little skip, and
suddenly, with great rapidity and no apparent effort, proceeded to ascend the precipice. He did not climb; he rose.
It was as if someone were hoisting him up from above and
he had merely to prevent himself from swinging out of the
perpendicular, by keeping contact with rocks in a few light
touches of foot and hand.

In just the same way, one after another, the Leblanc party
were whisked away out of sight. The stranger and I looked at
each other. 'Are you all right?' came reverberating down from
very far ahead. We began to climb. We climbed for about half
an hour up the cleft in the rock. Not once during that time
did we find a place where it was possible to rest or even to
stand still in any normal attitude. We just went on from foothold to foothold; our topis made it impossible to see more
than a foot or two above our heads. Suddenly we came on
the Leblanc party sitting on a ledge.

'You look hot,' said Mr Leblanc. 'I see you are not in training. You will find this most beneficial.'

As soon as we stopped climbing, our knees began to trem-
ble. We sat down. When the time came to start again, it was
quite difficult to stand up. Our knees seemed to be behaving
as they sometimes do in dreams, when they suddenly refuse

support in moments of pursuit by bearded women broad-casters.

'We thought it best to wait for you,' continued Mr Leblanc, 'because there is rather a tricky bit here. It is easy enough when you know the way, but you need someone to show you. I discovered it myself. I often go out alone in the evenings finding tricky bits. Once I was out all night, quite stuck. I thought I should be able to find a way when the moon rose. Then I remembered there was no moon that night. It was a very cramped position.'

The tricky bit was a huge overhanging rock with a crumbling flaky surface.

'It is really quite simple. Watch me and then follow. You put your right foot here . . .' – a perfectly blank, highly polished surface of stone – '. . . then rather slowly you reach up with your left hand until you find a hold. You have to stretch rather far . . . so. Then you cross your right leg under your left – this is the difficult part – and feel for a footing on the other side . . . With your right hand you just steady yourself . . . so.' Mr Leblanc hung over the abyss partly out of sight. His whole body seemed prehensile and tenacious. He *stood* there like a fly on the ceiling. 'That is the position. It is best to trust more to the feet than the hands – push up rather than pull down . . . you see the stone here is not always secure.' By way of demonstration he splintered off a handful of apparently solid rock from above his head and sent it

tinkling down to the road below. 'Now all you do is to shift
the weight from your left foot to your right, and swing yourself round . . . so.' And Mr Leblanc disappeared from view.

Every detail of that expedition is kept fresh in my mind
by recurrent nightmares. Eventually after about an hour's
fearful climb we reached the rim of the crater. The next stage
was a tramp across the great pit of loose cinders. Then the
ascent of the other rim, to the highest point of the peninsula.
Here we paused to admire the view, which was indeed most
remarkable; then we climbed down to the sea. Variety was
added to this last phase by the fact that we were now in the
full glare of the sun, which had been beating on the cliffs
from noon until they were blistering hot.

'It will hurt the hands if you hang on too long,' said Mr
Leblanc. 'One must jump on the foot from rock to rock like
the little goats.'

At last, after about three hours of it, we reached the beach.
Cars and servants were waiting. Tea was already spread; bathing-
dresses and towels laid out.

'We always bathe here, not at the club,' said Mr Leblanc.
'They have a screen there to keep out the sharks – while in
this bay, only last month, two boys were devoured.'

We swam out into the warm sea. An Arab fisherman,
hopeful of a tip, ran to the edge of the sea and began shouting to us that it was dangerous. Mr Leblanc laughed happily
and, with easy powerful strokes, made for the deep waters.

We returned to shore and dressed. My shoes were completely worn through, and there was a large tear in my shorts where I had slipped among the cinders and slid some yards. Mr Leblanc had laid out for him in the car a clean white suit, a shirt of green crêpe-de-Chine, a bow tie, silk socks, buckskin shoes, ivory hairbrushes, scent spray, and hair lotion. We ate banana sandwiches and drank very rich China tea.

For a little additional thrill on the way back, Mr Leblanc took the wheel of his car. I am not sure that that was not the most hair-raising experience of all.

Next day – Sunday, December 14th – intolerably stiff in every muscle, bruised, scratched, blistered by the sun, I set out for Lahej, where the Resident had arranged for me to spend two nights as the Sultan's guest to see the assembly of the tributary chiefs on Tuesday. This was to be the second of these assemblies. The first, held in the spring of the preceding year, had been an experiment in what is likely to prove an extremely important development in the Protectorate policy.

Until I came to Aden I did not realise that there was any particular policy there or any problems requiring solution. I saw a small red semi-circle on the map and supposed vaguely that it was a railed off, benevolently administered territory, sequestered from the troubles of the rest of Arabia, and overrun by mission schools, district officers, clinics, prevention-of-cruelty-to-animals inspectors, German and

Japanese commercial travellers, Fabian women collecting statistics and all the other concomitants of British imperialism. None of these things can be found anywhere in South Arabia. 'Protectorate' is one of the vaguest terms in the whole political jargon. In Zanzibar it means nothing less than a complete system of direct government; in Aden, until the last two or three years, it has merely meant the doling out or withholding of small stipends to the virtually independent tribal chiefs, who are bound to the Aden Government by thirty separate treaties. There has been no 'protection' in the ordinary sense of the word. At the beginning of the last war the entire territory, up to Khormaksar, was overrun by the Turks and remained in their hands until the Armistice. Even now there are seventy 'protected' subjects living as hostages in the hands of the Imam of Sana and large tracts of 'protected' territory paying him tribute. The boundaries shown in the atlas are practically meaningless; they are nowhere demarcated, but depend on traditional tribal holdings. The surrounding country is on all sides little known and inhospitable. The western border was defined by the 1903–4 boundary commission at the time when the Yemen was in Turkish hands. The Imam has never recognised that agreement and, in fact, openly and constantly violates it; to the north is the Rhub-al-Khali, where boundaries do not count. (It is interesting, at any rate for me, to think that, while Flight-Commander Vachell and I were looking at his large-scale service maps and at that great blank space in them, and he was describing some flights he had made skirting the edge and saying that of all uncharted parts of the world that was likely to keep its integrity the longest, during those very days Mr Bertram Thomas was setting out on his crossing.) On the north-east lies the Hadramaut, still, except for Mukulla, practically *terra incognita*. A recent explorer – Boscawen – reports a series of castles supporting a life of high luxury, inhabited by Arabs who have made fortunes in Java and the Malay States.

The Protectorate is the name for the thirty or so tribes living between these areas. They are entirely separate from Aden Settlement; their affairs are dealt with by the Colonial Office, while Aden itself is under the Bombay Presidency. The Resident at Aden is in charge of both. In the early days of the settlement the policy was initiated of paying money bribes to the immediate neighbours in return for a certain standard of good behaviour. This meant in all cases that they were to refrain from attacking the European and Indian settlers, and in five cases that they were to afford safe communication for the caravans coming down to the coast. It was a makeshift system from the start, but the endemic lethargy of the place prolonged it for nearly a century. Occasionally a more than usually vigorous administrator would attempt to put down internal hostilities by making the stipends conditional upon pacific behaviour, but, for the most part, the Residents seemed to have regarded residence as their primary duty.

Until the war, the pressure of Turkish expansion had been the chief consideration. When this was removed there seemed only two logical policies, either to abandon the Protectorate altogether, allow the Imam to overrun it, and make a single agreement with him for the safety of the settlement, or to institute direct administration. There were serious objections to both these courses; the first would be a breach of our treaty obligations – the Shafei sect of the protected tribes are irreconcilably hostile to the Zeidi highlanders – and the second certainly expensive and possibly unsuccessful.

A third course was proposed by Sir Stewart Symes,[1] and adopted as the policy of the British Government. This is to develop the Protectorate upon native and federal lines, resisting the consistent disintegrating tendency of Arab society by giving support always to paramount chiefs, and to unite the tribes into a single responsible body able to cooperate in frontier defence, and bound to the Aden Government by a single collective guarantee instead of the present hotchpotch of treaties. Under this régime Aden Settlement would become the cultural capital of the new State, and educational and medical service would eventually take the place of the old system of cash payments.

An essential part of this scheme is the institution of a *jurga*,

---

1. A few weeks after my visit Sir Stewart Symes left Aden to take up the Governorship of Tanganyika.

or tribal council, on the lines at present in operation in Baluchistan, which will act as a court of arbitration in internal disputes and as a single articulate body with whom the Aden Government can treat. The Sultan of Lahej is, by wealth and position, the natural president, *primus inter pares*, of this council. He is the only chief with prestige enough to assemble the others and with a palace to accommodate them.

The first council was held in the spring of 1929; most of the chiefs attended, bewildered and somewhat suspicious of the whole business. It was the first time in their lives, possibly the first time in the history of the tribes, that so many of them had sat down peaceably together. The new policy was explained to them in simple terms, and a treaty was drawn up and accepted, binding the signatories in general terms to cooperation and amicable relations. Conversations were held between the Resident, the Sultan of Lahej, and the various chiefs. They showed excusable anxiety about their pensions, but on the whole seemed interested. The success or failure of the assembly on Tuesday was regarded as an important indication of the practicability of making it a yearly function. The former signatory chiefs, and some others, had been invited to attend. The meeting was to be at the palace. A temporary British camp was being pitched two miles out of the town, where the Resident would be able to hold informal discussions with individual chiefs during the week.

This, very briefly, is the political situation in the Protectorate and the meaning of the assembly of chiefs, and that
was why, stiff and sore, I was being bumped along the track
from the peninsula to Lahej.

There was once a railway from Aden to Lahej, but it fell
out of use and had lately been demolished; a quay at the
docks was still littered with rusty rolling-stock and lengths
of rail. A young Scotsman was, in fact, at that moment staying at the hotel whose business was to see to their disposal.
I had some talk with him. His firm had bought the whole
concern, without seeing it, at a bargain price and then sent
him out to do the best he could with it. He was doing quite
well, he said, patiently selling it bit by bit in improbable
quarters of the world. No move had as yet been made to
replace it; we – Colonel Lake, the chief political officer, the
driver, and I – bounced along in the sand, in a six-wheel
army lorry, beside the remains of the track, which still clearly
showed the corrugations where the sleepers had lain. It took
us about two hours to reach the camp. The Aden Levy had
arrived the day before. Some neat little kitchens of grass and
wattles had been erected behind a sand dune, out of sight.
Great trouble had been taken with the alignment of the
camp; an avenue of signalling-flags led up to its centre;
the sites for the tents were symmetrically disposed round it.
The tents themselves were causing some trouble, particularly
a great cubic pavilion that was to be used for the Resident's

durbar; there was a high, hot wind blowing; grass and reeds had been scattered about to lay the driving sand, but with little success. Clouds of grit eddied everywhere.

Just as we arrived they got the big tent fixed at last; they stood back to admire it. The subaltern in charge came to greet us. 'Thank heavens we've got that done. We've been at it since five this morning. Now we can have a drink.'

While he was still speaking, the tent bellied, sagged, and fell; the patient little Arabs began their work again, laying foundations of stones, three feet deep, to hold the pegs in the loose sand.

We lunched in the mess-tent, dozed, and then, mounted on camels, Colonel Lake and I rode the remaining two miles into the town. I had already seen it from the air during a flight, frustrated by low clouds, which Vachell and I had attempted to make to Dhala. It was a typical Arab town of dun-coloured, flat-roofed houses and intricate alleyways. The palace was wholly European in conception, smaller than the Gebbi at Addis, but much better planned and better kept; there were pretty formal gardens in front of it, and all round the town lay bright green meadows and groves of coconut and date-palm. There was one large, lately redecorated mosque and the usual small shrines and tombs.

A power station has lately been built and most of the principal houses installed with electricity. This is naturally a matter for great pride and, to draw his visitors' attention more closely to the innovation, the sultan has conceived the rather unhappy plan of building the new guest-house immediately over the electric plant. Fortunately this was not yet finished, so that we were directed to the old guest-house, a pleasant, rather dilapidated villa of pseudo-European style, standing at the extremity of the town on the edge of the fields. Here Colonel Lake left me in the charge of the Arab butler, having elicited the fact that there were two other occupants of the house – German engineers in the sultan's employ. Except for these there were no Europeans of any kind in the town.

The furniture was very simple; in my room, a wash-hand stand with odd china, an iron bedstead with a mosquito-curtain and one collapsible, Hyde Park chair; round the walls were traces of a painted dado, representing looped and fringed curtains and gilt tassels; in the living-rooms, two tables, more Hyde Park chairs, and some iron rocking-chairs, which seem to play an essential part of hospitality in the East, as gilt chairs once did in London. There were also some personal possessions of the German engineers – two or three comic magazines of a year or two back, a fiddle, some tins of fruit and biscuits, Alpine photographs, a gramophone, an album containing photographs of male cinema-stars.

After about an hour they themselves arrived. They were very young men – both twenty-two, I learned later – and they had come in overalls straight from work; they spoke

English, one rather better than the other, but both very fluently, loudly, and unintelligibly. Their first concern was to apologise for their appearance. They would be ashamed to speak to me, they said, until they had washed and changed. They had fitted up a kind of shower-bath behind a curtain of sacking at the top of the stairs. Here they hid themselves and spluttered happily for some minutes, emerging later, naked, dripping, and better composed. They dried themselves, combed their hair, put on smart tropical suits, and called for dinner. They produced some bottled amstel from beneath their beds and put it under the shower-bath to cool, and opened a tin of greengages in my honour. They were a most friendly, generous pair.

Dinner consisted of a highly pungent meat stew and salad. The cooking was not good, they explained, and they suspected the butler of cheating the sultan and themselves by confiscating their rations and substituting inferior purchases of his own; however, it did not do to complain; they were well paid and could afford to supplement their meals with biscuits and beer and tinned fruit; they would probably be the ultimate losers in any conflict with the butler. I should find, they said, that their food would make me rather ill. At first they suffered continuously from dysentery and nettle-rash; also the mosquito-curtains were too short and were full of holes. I should probably get a touch of malaria. The salad, they said, helping themselves profusely, was full of typhus.

I retail this information simply and concisely as though it had come to me in so many words. As a matter of fact, it took the whole of dinner in telling, and half an hour or so afterwards. Both spoke simultaneously all the time, and, when the issues became confused, louder and louder. 'We know English so well because we always speak it with our Dutch friends at Aden,' they explained (but again at far greater length and with many misunderstandings and cross purposes). 'It was largely from them that we learned it.'

There were interruptions. Fairly frequently the light turned orange, flickered, and went out, on one occasion, for so long that we all set out to the power station to see what had happened. Just as we left the house, however, we saw the lights go up again, and returned to our conversation. 'Engineer', I realised, was a title covering a variety of functions. Three times messages came from the palace; once, to say that the water-closet had broken and that they were to come and mend it first thing in the morning; again, to say that one of Sultan Achmed's (the Sultan of Lahej's brother) new tractors was stuck in a watercourse; a third, to remark that the lights kept going out. All these things were duly noted down for their attention.

Next morning I had an audience with the sultan. His Highness was an impassive, middle-aged man, wearing semi-European clothes – turban, black frock coat, white linen trousers. As head of the Fadl family, the hereditary rulers of the Abdali tribe and, for a brief period, the former possessors of Aden, he holds by far the most influential position in the Protectorate. He is in close personal relationship with the Settlement Government and substantially supported by them.

At the time of our first occupation of Aden, the Fadl family had for about eighty years been independent of the Imam; their position, however, was precarious, and it was directly from them[1] that the Settlement Government inherited the futile system of purchasing the goodwill of the neighbouring tribes with regular monetary bribes. Their connection with the British Government has tended greatly to increase the family's wealth and stability and consequent prestige. They are, in fact, the only really secure house in Southern Arabia, and would have most to lose, of any of the Protectorate tribes, from Zeidi overlordship. There is no resident adviser at Lahej and no attempt at domestic control. Within his own territory the sultan's power is only limited by the traditional law of his own people.

We drank delicious coffee on the balcony overlooking the palace gardens and, with the aid of an interpreter, asked politely after each other's health and the health of our relatives. I commented on the striking modernity of his city – the electric light, the water-supply, the motor-buses; he remarked

1. Treaty between the Company and the Sultan of Lahej 1839 by which the Company made themselves responsible for stipends formerly paid by the sultan to the Fadhli, Yafai, Haushabi and Amiri.

how much more modern these things were in London. He said that the Resident told him I wrote books; that he had not himself written a book, but that his brother had written a very good one, which I must see before I left Lahej. Conversations through an interpreter always seem to me so artificial that it is hardly worth while thinking for anything to say. He asked after my comfort at the guest-house; I replied that it was luxury itself; he said not so luxurious as London. I was at the moment, just as the Germans had predicted, tortured with nettle-rash. I said that the tranquillity was greater than in London. He said that soon he would have more motor-buses. Then we took leave of each other and I was conducted to Sultan Achmed Fadl.

His Highness's brother lived in a small, balconied house on the further side of the main square. He was already receiving company. A British political officer was there, the subaltern who had supervised the collapse of the Resident's durbar tent, and the Haushabi sultan; a secretary was in attendance and numerous servants and guards sat about on the narrow staircase.

The Haushabi sultan was an important young man finely dressed and very far from sane. He sat in a corner giggling with embarrassment, and furtively popping little twigs of *khat* into his mouth. It was not often that his womenfolk allowed him to leave his own district. Sultan Achmed was a good-looking man of about forty, with high, intellectual forehead and exquisite manners; he spoke English well. His habit of life was pious and scholarly. He had private estates, almost as large as his brother's, whose cultivation he supervised himself, experimenting eagerly with new methods of irrigation, new tractors and fertilisers, new kinds of crops – a complete parallel to the enlightened landed gentleman of eighteenth-century England.

He showed me his book: a history of the Fadl family from the remotest times until the death of his father (unfortunately shot by a British sentry during the evacuation of Lahej before the Turkish advance in 1915). It was written in exquisite script, illuminated with numerous genealogies in red and black. He hoped to have a few copies printed for distribution among his friends and relatives, but he did not think it was likely to command a wide sale.

He suggested a drive, and went to change. His motoring-costume consisted of a grey overcoat, white shorts, khaki stockings, parti-coloured black-and-white shoes, and a grey silk veil. When he gave orders, his servants kissed his knees, and, whenever we stopped during the drive, passers-by hurried to salute him in the same way. His car was not new – I think it must have been one of those devised by the German mechanics from the débris of former accidents – but it carried a crest of ostrich plumes on the bonnet and an armed guard beside the chauffeur. We drove to his country house a mile or two away and walked for some time in his gardens –

shrubs flowering in the shade of coconut-palms by the bank of a stream. He ordered a bunch of flowers to be prepared for me, and the gardeners brought a vast bundle of small, sweet-smelling roses and some great spear-shaped white flowers, sheathed in barbed leaves, which gave out a scent of almost stifling richness, reputed throughout Arabia, so the Germans told me later, to act upon women as an aphrodisiac. He also gave me twelve gourds of Dhala honey, eight of which were subsequently stolen by the butler at the guest-house, who thus, with unconscious kindness, relieved me of a particularly unmanageable addition to my luggage, without my incurring any possible self-reproach on grounds of ingratitude.

That afternoon I visited the camp where all the tents were at last firmly in position, and in the evening I sat with the Germans, gradually disentangling from their flow of sound an outline of their really remarkable careers. They had left school at Munich when they were eighteen and, together with a large number of boys of their year, had determined to seek their fortunes. Accordingly they had split up into pairs, made a solemn leavetaking, and scattered all over the globe. They had no money, their only assets being a sketchy knowledge of practical mechanics and, they said, a natural gift for languages. They had worked their way doing odd jobs at garages, through Spain and North Africa to Abyssinia, with the vague intention of sometime reaching India. Two years before at Berbera they had heard that the Sultan of Lahej had just expelled his French engineer for dishonest practices; they had crossed the gulf on the chance of getting the job, had got it, and remained there ever since. They undertook every kind of work, from the mending of punctures in his Highness's tyres to the construction of a ferro-concrete dam on the wadi and the irrigation of his entire estates. They had charge of the electric plant and the water-supply of the town; they mended the firearms of the palace guard; they drew up the plans and supervised the construction of all new buildings; they advised on the choice of agricultural machinery; with their own hands they installed the palace water-closet – the only thing of its kind in the whole of Southern Arabia. When not otherwise engaged, they put in their time patching up abandoned army lorries and converting them into motor-buses. Their only fear was that the sultan might take it into his head to procure an aeroplane; that, they felt, would almost certainly lead to trouble. Meanwhile, they were as happy as the day was long; they would have to move on soon, however; it would not do to risk Stagnation of the Spirit.

Sultan Achmed combined his gentler pursuits with the office of commander-in-chief of the army, and early next morning he was busy inspecting the guard of honour and inducing a high degree of uniformity in their equipment. Long before the Resident was due to arrive they were drawn up in the palace courtyard, arranged like strawberries on a coster's barrow, with the most presentable to the fore. The chiefs had been arriving on horses and camels throughout the preceding afternoon, and had been quartered according to their rank in various houses about the town. They formed a very remarkable spectacle as they assembled among the fumed-oak furniture and plush upholstery of the sultan's state drawing-room. No one except the Fadl family and their Ministers had attempted European dress. They wore their best and most brilliant robes, and in most cases finely jewelled swords of considerable antiquity. They talked very little to each other, but stood about awkwardly, waiting for the Resident's entry, mutually suspicious, like small boys during the first half-hour of a children's party. Most of them, in spite of interminable genealogies, lived, in their own homes, a life of almost squalid simplicity, and they were clearly overawed by the magnificence of Lahej; some from the remoter districts were bare-footed and they trod the Brussels carpets with very uncertain steps; embarrassment gave them a pop-eyed look, quite unlike the keen, hawk faces of cinema sheiks. While we were waiting, I was introduced to each in turn, and through my interpreter, had a few words with them, asking whether they had had a long journey and what the prospects were for the crops and grazing-land. I was much struck by the extreme youth of the assembly; except for the old Amir of Dhala, few of the chiefs seemed to be much older than myself, while there were one or two small children among them. This I learned was a matter of policy. The tendency of Arab communities is always towards the multiplication of political units, so that the death of a chief is invariably the occasion for discord and disintegration, with consequent neglect and damage of communal property. To mitigate this evil a practice of post-remogeniture has arisen among those tribes in which, as is usually the case, the chieftainship is elective within the ruling family, by choosing the youngest eligible male and thus postponing as far as possible the recurrence of the emergency.

As soon as the Aden party arrived we took our places in the council-room, and the chiefs were formally announced one after another in order of precedence; each in turn shook hands with the Resident and then sat down in the chair assigned to him. Some were at first too shy to go the whole length of the room, and tried to get away with little bows from the door; their companions, however, prodded them on, and they came lolloping up with downcast eyes to give very hurried greeting and then shoot for a chair. It was all very much like the prize-giving after village sports, with Sir Stewart as the squire's wife and the Sultan of Lahej as the vicar, benevolently but firmly putting the tenants' children through their paces. It was hard to believe that each of them could lead a troop of fighting men into the field and administer an ancient and intricate law to a people of perhaps fifteen hundred, perhaps twenty thousand souls.

The Sultan of Lahej made a little speech, in Arabic, opening the conference; then Sir Stewart Symes, first in English and then in Arabic, reminded his audience of the purpose of the meeting and outlined the chief local events of the past eighteen months, explaining the motives and activities of the Aden Government. Little was said of a question that was clearly in everyone's thoughts – the Imam of Sana.

Round this somewhat mysterious figure centres one of the chief problems of immediate practical importance in Arabia. Civil and religious prestige, mingling indistinguishably as they do in Mohammedan communities, have combined to give him a unique position in local politics. He traces his descent directly from the Zeidi Imam who, in A.D. 900, migrated south from Iraq and established himself in the Yemen highlands. From time to time, ancestors of his have held practically all the territory from the Hejaz to the Hadramaut. In 1630 they defeated the Turks and became paramount over most of the tribes now included in the protectorate; towards the middle of the eighteenth century there were a series of successful Shafei risings in the lowlands, and, throughout the second half of the nineteenth century, Turkish expansion again confined them to the hills. The present Imam led a revolt in 1904 which was easily subdued by the Turks, and from then until 1918 he accepted a mediatised status, confining himself to the Yemen proper, and resigning claims to authority over the Shafei tribes. Immediately after the war, however, he began a policy of penetration, occupying Shafei towns beyond the frontier agreed on by the 1903–4 Anglo-Turkish boundary commission. In 1928 the British Government were induced to move, and the local Air Force units, cooperating with the local tribesmen, easily forced the Zeidi to evacuate Dhala and other 'protected' areas. Before the process was complete, however, instructions were issued from London to cease action, leaving large Shafei districts and many hostages in the Imam's hands. Since then there have been no official negotiations between the two parties. The Imam's political policy is compromised by his religious position; like the Pope, he shares the embarrassments with the advantages of supernatural sanction. Once having laid claim to the Protectorate, he cannot recede except under superior force, and that the London Government are unwilling to employ. The Imam remains at Sana in rather anxious seclusion; two unofficial British travellers were lately received by him, and entrusted with an embassy offering the very comic terms that the British should renounce all treaty obligations with the Shafei tribes, in return for which the Imam was willing to allow them possession of Aden and Perim, provided that it was officially and openly admitted that they were there on his sufferance. The British Government have adopted the superficially dignified attitude of complete aloofness, while the Imam's private troubles pile up. He has a serious Shafei problem within his own dominions round Hodeida, and hostilities are threatening with his Wahabite neighbour, Ibn Saud of the Hejaz. Sooner or later he is bound to sue for British friendship. All this is perfectly satisfactory to the Colonial Office at Whitehall, but it is less easy to induce the actual sufferers in Arabia to take a long-sighted view of the situation. The old Amir of Dhala's brother is a hostage at Sana. The Audli country is in two parts; the northern is a fertile plateau, the southern is desert; the Zeidi are in possession of the entire northern plateau, taxing the people and consuming the crops; the Audli sultan is ten years old – a child, incidentally, of some beauty and exquisite gravity, who sat beside his uncle throughout the conference, superbly dressed, his eyes lined with indigo. There was one old sheik who did not attend the conference this year; he had just heard that his only son, a hostage in the Imam's hands, had been killed in the collapse of the prison roof. 'Trusteeship of weaker races' is a phrase popularly current in Whitehall, where its application involves the bankruptcy of pioneer, white settlers in Africa; when the same idea implies the risk of parliamentary criticism, 'Jingoism' takes its place.

It is very surprising to discover the importance which politics assume the moment one begins to travel. In England they have become a hobby for specialists – at best a technical question in economics, at worst a mere accumulation of gossip about thoroughly boring individuals. One can trip about France or Italy with the utmost delight and profit without holding any views on *L'Action française* or Fascism. Outside Europe one cannot help being a politician if one is at all interested in what one sees; political issues are implicit in everything, and I make no apology for their occasional appearance in these pages. I went abroad with no particular views about empire and no intention of forming any. The problems were so insistent that there was no choice but to become concerned with them.

When the speeches were over, we adjourned to the drawing-room and talked until luncheon. Only the English party and the prime minister lunched with the sultan. It was a very fine banquet, including fresh asparagus served with onion sauce; we drank lemon squash as befitted a Mohammedan function. After luncheon I took leave of the sultan and returned with the Aden party to the settlement. I wish I could have stayed longer. On the next two days the Resident was to hold his durbar in the camp, interviewing those of the chiefs who had matters to discuss with him in private. After that there was to be a day when no British would visit Lahej, in the hope that the chiefs might begin to form understandings with one another and share each other's problems. On the last day there was to be a garden-party at

the palace. I wish I could have stayed, but my fortnight at
Aden was up. The *Explorateur Grandidier* was due next day, sailing for Zanzibar; if I missed her there was another fortnight
to wait. It was six weeks since I had had any mail; I had
arranged for everything to be sent to Zanzibar. My plans for
the future were still vague, but that tight-lipped young man
at Harar had set me considering the idea of crossing Africa
to the west coast. And so, what with one thing and another,
I decided to move on.

Two

Everyone admitted that it was an unfortunate time to visit Zanzibar. Usually in the tropics, if one remarks on the temperature, the inhabitants assume an air of amused tolerance and say, 'You find this hot? You ought to see what it's like in such a month.' But December in Zanzibar is recognised as a bad season.

Throughout my stay I am obsessed by heat; I see everything through a mist, vilely distorted like those gross figures that loom at one through the steam of a Turkish bath.

I live at the English Club. Every day, soon after dawn, I am awakened by the heat; I lie there under my mosquito-net streaming with sweat, utterly exhausted; I take time summoning enough resolution to turn the pillow dry side up; a boy comes in with tea and a mango; I lie there uncovered for a little while, dreading the day. Everything has to be done very slowly. Presently I sit limply in a hip-bath of cold water; I know that before I am dry of the water I shall again be damp with sweat. I dress gradually. One wears long trousers, coat, shirt, socks, suspenders, bow tie, buckskin shoes, everything in this town. Half-way through dressing I cover my head with eau-de-quinine and sit under the electric fan. I do this several times during the day. They are the only tolerable moments. I go up to breakfast. A Goan steward offers me bacon and eggs, fish, marmalade. I eat *papai* – an odious vegetable, tasteless and greasy; it is good for one. I go up to the library and read local history. I try to smoke. The fan blows fragments of burning tobacco over my clothes; the bowl of the pipe is too hot to hold. Through the window a very slight breeze carries up from the streets a reek of cloves, copra, and rotten fruit. A ship has been in the night before. I send a boy to the bank to inquire after my mail; there is still nothing. I make notes about the history of Zanzibar; the ink runs in little puddles of sweat that fall on to the page; I leave hot thumb-prints on the history-book. The plates have all come loose and the fan scatters them about the library. Luncheon is early. I usually sit with a young official who is living at the club during his wife's absence at home. I tease him by putting on an earnest manner and asking him for information which I know he will be unable to give me – 'Are there any reciprocal rights at law between French subjects in Zanzibar and British subjects in Madagascar? Where, in the Protectorate Budget, do the rents appear, paid for the sultan's possessions on the mainland? What arrangement was made between the Italian Government and the sultan about the cession of the Somaliland littoral below the River Juba?' – or questions which I know will embarrass him – 'Were the commercial members of Council in favour of the loan from the Zanzibar Treasury to the Government of Kenya? Is it a fact that the sultan pays for his own postage account and the Resident does not; is it a fact that the sultan has money invested abroad which the administration want to trace?' He is very patient and promises to ring up the solicitor-general that afternoon and get the facts I want. After luncheon I go to bed. At two-forty exactly, every afternoon, the warm little wind that has been blowing from the sea, drops. The sudden augmentation of heat wakes me up. I have another bath. I cover my head with eau-de-quinine and sit under the fan. Tea. Sometimes I go to Benediction in the cathedral, where it is cool. Sometimes my official takes me for a drive into the country, through acres of copra-palm and clove-trees and tidy little villages, each with police station and clinic. Sometimes I receive a call from a Turk whom I met on the ship coming here; he talks of the pleasures of Nice and the glories of Constantinople before the war; he wears close-cropped hair and a fez; he cannot wear his fez in Nice, he tells me, because they take him for an Egyptian and charge him excessively for everything. We drink lemon squash together and plan a journey in the Hejaz. 'We will ride and ride,' he says, 'until our knees are cut and bleeding.' He is very interesting about Mohammedanism, which he seems to regard as a family affair of his own, rather as Old Catholics in England regard the Universal Church. It is interesting, too, to discuss European history with an intelligent man who has learned it entirely from a Mohammedan point of view. The warmth of my admiration for Armenians clearly shocks him, but he is too polite to say so. Instead, he tells me of splendid tortures inflicted on them by his relatives.

Dinner on the club terrace; it is a little cooler now; one can eat almost with pleasure. Often, in the evening, we go out for a drive or visit a *ngoma*. Once I went to the cinema, where, quite unlike Aden, the audience was wide awake – mainly composed of natives, shrieking hysterically at the eccentricities of two drunken Americans. The *ngomas* are interesting. They are Swahili dances, originally, no doubt, of ritual significance, but nowadays performed purely for recreation. Like most activities, native or immigrant, in Zanzibar, they are legalised, controlled, and licensed. A list is kept in the police station of their place and date; anyone may attend. Once or twice, teams of fine negroes from the mainland made their appearance, and gave a performance more varied and theatrical than the local one. Missionaries look askance at the entertainments, saying that they induce a state of excitement subversive of the moral law. One dance we attended took place in absolute darkness; we were even asked to put out our cigars. It was, as far as we could see, a kind of blind-man's-buff; a man stood in the centre enveloped in an enormous conical extinguisher made of thatched grass, while the rest of the company capered round him, making derisive cries, beating tins and challenging him to catch them. The tufted top of his hood could just be seen pitching and swaying across the sky. On another occasion a particularly good mainland party – from somewhere below Tanga I was told – brought a band of four or five tom-tom players. It was odd to see these men throwing back their heads and rolling their eyes and shoulders like trick drummers in a Paris orchestra.

We made an excursion into the brothel quarter, which in Burton's time, and for a generation after, was one of the most famous in the East. Now, however, there is nothing to see or to tempt the young official from domesticity. It is squalid and characterless. Moreover, at the sight of us the women ran into their houses or hid in their yards. It was assumed at once that we were spies, not customers. This is creditable or not to the character of British officialdom, according as you like to look on it.

The only thing which does not appear to be under the benevolent eye of the administrator in Zanzibar is witchcraft, which is still practised surreptitiously on a very large scale. At one time, Zanzibar and Pemba – particularly the latter island – were the chief centres of black art in the whole coast, and novices would come from as far as the great lakes to graduate there. Even from Haiti, it is said, witch doctors will occasionally come to probe the deepest mysteries of voodoo. Nowadays everything is kept hidden from the Europeans, and even those who have spent most of their lives in the country have only now and then discovered hints of the wide, infinitely ramified cult which still flourishes below the surface. No one doubts, however, that it does flourish, and it seems appropriate that it should have its base here in this smug community.

One day my Turkish friend and I drove out to tea at Bububu. This name had lived in my mind ever since a question was asked in the House of Commons about the future of the Bububu railway. I had hoped that perhaps one day Mr Sutro might choose the Zanzibar–Bububu line for a Railway Club dinner. But alas, like the Lahej railway, it has now been abolished and the scraps sold for what they will fetch. One can still discern traces of the impermanent way among the copra-palms on the outskirts of the town.

The village and surrounding estate belong to a stout, bald, very cheerful Arab, a cousin of the sultan's. He drove us out from Zanzibar, pointing on the way to the derelict villas of various of his relatives. His own was far from neat, but large, and set in a beautiful walled garden full of fountains, many of which had been made to work in our honour. The furniture was a curious medley of pseudo-Oriental – which Orientals seem greatly to prefer to the products of their own craftsmen – and pseudo-European. We sat outside on the terrace in the shade of a dense mango-tree, perched on the inevitable Hyde Park chairs, and ate biscuits and preserved ginger. Whisky and soda had been produced for me, the Turk conscientiously confining himself to tea. My host seemed fairly certain that I was in some way connected with the Government – the fact that I bore no official rank making my mission the more important – and he was at some pains to express his dearest loyalty to the British administration. According to the gracious Arab custom, we were loaded with flowers on our return.

I think that, more than the climate, it is the absence of any kind of political issue which makes Zanzibar so depressing. There are no primary problems at all; such difficulties as there are, are mere matters of the suitable adjustment of routine. There are no perceptible tendencies among the people towards nationalisation or democracy. The sultan is the model of all that a figurehead should be; a man of dignified bearing and reputable private life. He has no exclusively valid claim to his office; the British Government put him there, and they pay him a sufficient proportion of his revenue to enable him to live in a modest degree of personal comfort and at the same time support a system of espionage wide enough to keep him in touch with the doings of his protectors. The two main industries of the islands, cloves and copra, are thoroughly prosperous compared with any other form of agriculture on the East African coast. Law and order are better preserved than in many towns in the British Isles. The medical and hygienic services are admirable; miles of excellent roads have been made. The administration is self-supporting. The British Government takes nothing out of the island. Instead, we import large numbers of well-informed, wholly honest members of our unemployed middle class to work fairly hard in the islanders' interest for quite small wages. Gay, easily intelligible charts teach the Swahili peasants how best to avoid hookworm and elephantiasis. Instead of the cultured, rather decadent aristocracy of the Oman Arabs, we have given them a caste of just, soap-loving young men with Public School blazers. And these young men have made the place safe for the Indians.

British imperialism takes on an odd complexion in some parts of the world. In East Africa its impetus was neither military nor commercial, but evangelical. We set out to stop the slave-trade. For this reason, and practically no other, public opinion forced on the Government the occupation of Zanzibar and the construction of the Uganda railway. In the last two decades of the nineteenth century, zealous congregations all over the British Isles were organising bazaars and sewing-parties with the single object of stamping out Arabic culture in East Africa. There was an alliance between Church and State as cordial as it always should have been, but rarely was, between Papacy and Empire. The Mohammedans were to be driven out with the Martini rifle and Gatling gun; the pagans were to be gently elevated with the hymn-book.

The firearms did their work, and a constant supply of

curates flowed to the mission-field. But for every curate there were a dozen grubby amateur law-givers. Throughout Zanzibar and Pemba, Indians have obtained control of the entire retail trade; almost without exception every shop – from the tailor who makes mess-jackets for the Resident's ADC to the petty grocer in a tin shed up country who cheats the peasant out of a few pice in the sale of cigarettes – is in Indian hands. The British bankruptcy law seems to have been devised expressly for Hindu manipulation. From Zanzibar as far as the lakes, every magistrate tells the same story, of Indian traders who set up shop without capital, obtain goods on credit, transmit money to India, go bankrupt for the value of their original stock, and then start again. No Arab or European can compete with them, because they can subsist on a standard of living as low as the natives. But with this difference. What among the natives is a state of decent, primitive simplicity is squalor among the Indian immigrants, because where the natives are bound by tribal loyalties and wedded to their surroundings by a profound system of natural sanctity, the East African Indians are without roots or piety. More than this, in the islands (but not to any important extent on the mainland) the Indians are gradually obtaining possession of the soil. The Arabs are by nature a hospitable and generous race and are 'gentlemen' in what seems to me the only definable sense, that they set a high value on leisure; deprived by the Pax Britannica of their traditional recreations, these qualities tend to degenerate into extravagance and laziness, as they do in any irresponsible aristocracy. Following the normal European rake's progress, they run into debt, mortgage their estates. This, under the protection of British law, has been the Indians' opportunity. The courts are continually busy with applications by Indians for possession of Arab property. The former landed gentry either take up positions as managers on their old estates or else drift to the town, where they hang about the cafés in tattered finery, offering their services as guides to tourists. An English legal officer told me he was convinced that, in the great majority of the cases he tried, the money advanced was a very small fraction of the value of the property. What could one do? – the Arabs signed anything without reading it.

No doubt the process was inevitable; it is the Arabs' fault; they have failed to adapt themselves to the economic revolution caused by the suppression of the slave-trade, and they must consequently be submerged. There was nothing the British could have done about it. All this is true, but the fact remains that if the British had not come to East Africa the change would not have taken place. We came to establish a Christian civilisation and we have come very near to establishing a Hindu one. We found an existing culture which, in spite of its narrowness and inflexibility, was essentially decent and valuable; we have destroyed that – or, at least, attended at its destruction – and in its place fostered the growth of a mean and dirty culture. Perhaps it is not a matter for censure; but it is a matter for regret.

So far I have said nothing about the town.

Seen from the sea, as one approaches it, it is pretty, but quite unremarkable. Palm-groves stretch out on either side; the town looks very small and flat. There are no domes or minarets, as the puritanical tenets of the particular sect that is locally espoused forbid display of this kind. The chief houses on the front are the sultan's palace and the 'House of Wonders' – the translation of the Arabic name for the municipal offices; there is a good staircase in this building, but neither it nor the palace show anything of interest from outside. The plan of the town is infinitely involved, a tangle of alleys, winding in and out, turning in their course and coming surprisingly to dead ends or leading back to their points of departure. The houses are solid Arab-work of the seventeenth and eighteenth centuries, mostly with fine doorways of carved wood and massive doors studded with brass bosses. Almost all the interiors have admirable staircases. One excellent quality commends this system of town planning – everything is extremely compact. In towns such as Nairobi, Mombasa, or Kampala, which have grown up since the introduction of hygiene, one is continually involved in expensive taxi rides. At Zanzibar the residency, cathedral, club, bank, post office, hotel, offices, and shops are all within five minutes' walk of one another. The town is, I suppose, as good an example of Arabic eighteenth-century architecture as survives intact anywhere. Liner passengers, trotting round in rickshaws, are apt to attribute greater antiquity to it. I met at least one lady who associated it with biblical time.

Zanzibar in the time of Burton must have been a city of great beauty and completeness. Now there is not a single Arab in any of the great Arab houses; there are, instead, counting-houses full of Indian clerks or flats inhabited by cosy British families and scattered with Egyptian hieroglyphics in appliqué embroidery, Benares brass, cane chairs, school groups, 'finds' from the bazaars, and European children's toys. The alleys, at least in the European quarter, are absurdly clean, and memsahibs go hooting down them in Morris two-seaters.

The modern architecture has mostly been rather happy. The residency and the museum – an interesting collection created and preserved by the delightful Dr Spurier – are the work of an amateur, rather over-impressed by the glamour of his surroundings. My Turkish friend, indeed, could not for some time be persuaded that the museum was not the tomb of some notable, and was accustomed to make appropriate devotions as he passed, until I drew him inside and pointed out the bottled snakes, the decorations of the late sultan, the autographed letters of felicitation from Queen Victoria, Livingstone's medicine chest (which, by the way, contained practically no quinine, but an enormous variety of pharmaceutically valueless poisons), propagandist photographs of unvaccinated children suffering from smallpox, and other objects of interest. The latest buildings, however, designed by the present official architect, seemed to me very good indeed, combining great economy and restraint with a delicate receptiveness to local influences. He has not yet had scope, however, for any work requiring high imagination. It will be a great pity if, while he holds his office, some fanatic does not succeed in destroying the sultan's boring nineteenth-century palace, so that he may have the rebuilding of it. Neither cathedral is of much artistic interest.

I went to Pemba for two nights. It is all cloves, coconuts, and tarmac, very much like the interior of Zanzibar. A small steamboat, the *Halifa*, makes a weekly journey to the north end of the island and back; the crossing takes a night. I disembarked at Mkoani, a green hillside scattered with bungalows; the water below the little landing-stage was clearer than I ever saw sea-water – every pebble, fathoms down, perfectly visible. I drove with the provincial commissioner to Weti, stopping to pay various calls on the way at Chake-Chake and a model estate managed by a community of Quakers. A delightful dinner that night with the doctor and his wife; no nonsense about stiff shirts and mess-jackets; we dined in pyjamas in a garden where preparations were being made for a Christmas-party. This was the only household in the island which possessed an electric-light plant, and the best was being made of it with globes swung from the trees. Next day – Christmas Eve – I sailed back to Chake-Chake, bathed in a party, went to cocktails at two bungalows, and dinner at a third, where a highly acrimonious dispute broke out late in the evening about the allotment of Christmas presents. My hosts were two elderly bachelors. They were giving a joint Christmas-party to the European children of the island, and a fine heap of toys had arrived for them in the *Halifa* for distribution to their guests. They rehearsed the business with chairs for children. 'This will do for So-and-So's little boy,' and 'This for So-and-So's girl,' and 'Have the So-and-So's got two children or three?' At first it was all very harmonious and Dickensian. Then suspicion of favouritism arose over the allocation of a particularly large, brightly painted india-rubber ball. 'Mary ought to have it; she's a sweet little thing.' 'Peter's brother has just gone to school in England. He's terribly lonely, poor kiddy.' The ball was put first on one dump, then on the other; sometimes it rolled off and bounced between them. 'Sweet little thing' and 'Lonely kiddy' became battle-cries as the big ball was snatched backwards and forwards. It was an odd sight to see these two hot men struggling over the toy. Presently came the inevitable 'All right. Do as you like. I wash my hands of the whole thing. I won't come to the party.' Renunciation was immediately mutual. There was a sudden reversal of the situation; each party tried to force the ball upon the other one's candidate. I cautiously eschewed any attempts at arbitration. Finally peace was made. I forget on what terms, but, as far as I remember, the ball was given to a third child and all the other heaps were despoiled to compensate Mary and Peter. They certainly came very well out of the business. Later that evening I went back to the *Halifa*. Some of my new friends came to see me off. We woke up the Goan steward and persuaded him to make lemon squash for us. Then we wished one another a happy Christmas, for it was past midnight, and parted. Early next morning we sailed for Zanzibar, arriving at tea-time. My mail had not yet come.

Christmas seemed very unreal divorced from its usual Teutonic associations of yule logs, reindeer, and rum punch. A few of the Indian storekeepers in the main street had decked their windows with tinsel, crackers, and iridescent artificial snow; there was a homely crèche in the cathedral; beggars appeared with the commendation 'Me velly Clistian boy'; there was a complete cessation of the little club life that had flourished before. I thought that I should have to spend Christmas Night alone, but Dr Spurier introduced me to a delightful party in a flat near the wharf.

Eventually the mail arrived, and I was able to leave for Kenya. I took an almost empty Italian liner named the *Mazzini*. Her main business is done between Genoa and Mombasa. She then makes a week's round trip to Zanzibar, Dar-es-Salaam, and back to Mombasa, and so to Europe. Her few passengers were nearly all restful people taking a few days' holiday on the water. The best thing about this ship was a nice old cinematograph; the worst was a plague of small black beetles which overran the cabins and died in vast numbers in the baths. An English lady declared that she had been severely stung by one in the back of the neck – but I find this difficult to believe. She and her husband were from Nairobi. It was the first time they had seen the sea since their arrival in the country eleven years before. The husband was a manufacturer of bricks. The trouble about his bricks, he said, was that they did not last very long; sometimes they crumbled away before they had been laid; but he was hopeful of introducing a new method before long.

We stopped at Dar-es-Salaam. It was hideously hot and there seemed little of interest in the town – some relics of Arab and German occupation, a rash of bungalows, a corrugated-iron bazaar full of Indians. I visited the agent of the Belgian Congo and explained that I had an idea of returning to Europe by way of the west coast. He was sympathetic to the idea and told me of an air service running weekly between Albertville and Boma; the fare was negligible, the convenience extreme. He showed me a timetable of the flight. It was two years old. He had not yet received the new one, but, he assured me, I could be confident that any changes that might have been made would be changes for the better. I believed him.

On the last day of the year we arrived at Mombasa. I had

spent a pleasant evening there on my way down. It is a green island, linked to the mainland by a bridge. The English have converted it into a passable reproduction of a garden-city. Kilindini docks lie at some distance outside the town. They are very grand – far finer than anything I had seen since Port Said: there is a Portuguese fort, bits of an Arab quarter, a club, golf links, bathing-beach, some hotels. On this particular morning, however, my whole time was occupied with the immigration officers.

We were called up to interview them in the saloon. They were a pair of chubby nonentities who at home might have secured posts at an inferior private school or in the counting-house of some wholesale drapery business in the Midlands. In Mombasa they were people of authority and very ready to show it. I presented a passport in which a former foreign secretary requested and required in the name of His Majesty that all whom it might concern should allow me to pass freely without let or hindrance and should afford me any assistance and protection of which I might stand in need. I did not need very much. All I wanted was to catch the 4.30 train to Nairobi. On the face of it, it seemed a simple business. Not at all. The foreign secretary's commendation did not seem to be wholly intelligible. I was given a form to fill in. Why was I coming to Kenya? For how long? Whom did I know there? Where was I going to stay? How much money had I got? Under what other aliases was I accustomed

to travel? Of what crimes had I been convicted in what coun-
tries? I completed the form and handed it over. They read
my replies, shaking their heads significantly at one another,
and asked me to wait behind while they dealt with the less
suspicious passengers. Presently they tackled me again. What
proofs had I of the truth of my statements? I went below,
unpacked my luggage and brought up letters of credit for a
little under two hundred pounds, and introductions to the
colonial secretary and the apostolic delegate. My inquisitors
held a whispered conference. Then they said that they
required a deposit of fifty pounds. Was this obligatory on all
visitors? No, but my replies had been unsatisfactory. In what
way unsatisfactory? At about this stage an element of mutual
dislike became apparent in the tone of our conversation.

'You say that you intend to remain here *about* three weeks.
Why do you not say exactly?'

'Because I have not yet decided. It may be five weeks. It
may be two. It depends how I like the country.'

'You say your address at Nairobi is "uncertain". What do
you mean by that?'

'I mean that I do not know. I have wired to a friend' –
naming the chief ADC at Government House – 'asking him
to engage a room for me. He has promised to get me one at
Muthaiga Club if it is possible. As it is race week there will
probably be some difficulty. I shall either be there or at Torr's
Hotel. I shall not know which until I reach Nairobi.'

More mutterings. Then:

'Have you got fifty pounds on you in East African currency?'

'No, I can give you a cheque.'

'That will not do. We shall hold your luggage and passport until you pay us fifty pounds in notes.'

'When shall I get it back?'

'When you leave the country.'

'But I shall be leaving through Uganda.'

'You must report to the emigration officer. He will write for it.'

'That will take some time?'

'Probably about a week.'[1]

'You mean that I shall have to wait a week at the frontier station.'

'Yes, that is what we mean.'

I drove into the town, cashed a cheque and returned to Kilindini. The immigration officers had now left the ship. I drove back to their office in the town, then back to Kilindini with their permission to land, then back to the town with my luggage.

That is how I spent my morning.

And so I entered Kenya fully resolved to add all I could to the already extensive body of abusive literature that has grown up round that much misunderstood dependency.

---

1. As it turned out, the money was eventually refunded to me in London towards the middle of April.

Three

But my ill temper gradually cooled as the train, with periodic derailments (three to be exact, between Mombasa and Nairobi) climbed up from the coast into the highlands. In the restaurant car that evening I sat opposite a young lady who was on her way to be married. She told me that she had worked for two years in Scotland Yard and that that had coarsened her mind; but since then she had refined it again in a bank at Dar-es-Salaam. She was glad to be getting married as it was impossible to obtain fresh butter in Dar-es-Salaam.

I awoke during the night to draw up my blanket. It was a novel sensation, after so many weeks, not to be sweating. Next morning I changed from white drill to grey flannel. We arrived in Nairobi a little before lunch time. I took a taxi out to Muthaiga Club. There was no room for me there, but the secretary had been told of my coming and I found I was already a temporary member. In the bar were several people I had met in the *Explorateur Grandidier*, and some I knew in London. They were drinking pink gin in impressive quantities. Someone said, 'You mustn't think Kenya is always like this.' I found myself involved in a luncheon-party. We went on together to the Races. Someone gave me a cardboard disc to wear in my buttonhole; someone else, called Raymond, introduced me to a bookie and told me what horses to back. None of them won. When I offered the bookie some money he said in rather a sinister way, 'Any friend of Mr de Trafford's is a friend of mine. We'll settle up at the end of the meeting.'

Someone took me to a marquee where we drank champagne. When I wanted to pay for my round the barman gave me a little piece of paper to sign and a cigar.

We went back to Muthaiga and drank champagne out of a silver cup which someone had just won.

Someone said, 'You mustn't think Kenya is always like this.'

There was a young man in a sombrero hat, trimmed with snake skin. He stopped playing dice, at which he had just dropped twenty-five pounds, and asked me to come to a dinner-party at Torr's. Raymond and I went back there to change.

On the way up we stopped in the bar to have a cocktail. A man in an orange shirt asked if either of us wanted a fight. We both said we did. He said, 'Have a drink instead.'

That evening it was a very large dinner-party, taking up all one side of the ballroom at Torr's. The young lady next to me said, 'You mustn't think that Kenya is always like this.'

After some time we went on to Muthaiga.

There was a lovely American called Kiki, whom I had

met before. She had just got up. She said, 'You'll like Kenya. It's always like this.'

Next morning I woke up in a very comfortable bedroom; the native boy who brought my orange juice said I was at Torr's.

I had forgotten all about Mombasa and the immigration officers.

Another side of Nairobi life: I sit at a table in the offices of the Indian Association, talking to the Indian leaders. They are named Mr Isher Dass, Mr Varma, and Mr Shams-ud-Deen. Mr Isher Dass is very conciliatory; he thanks me often for my open-minded attitude; he says that he hopes my book will be unlike *Mother India*. 'Quite unlike,' I assure him. Mr Varma is very pugnacious; he smokes cigars all the time; bangs the table and snarls. He says that colour prejudice in Kenya has come to such a pass that Indians are made to share the same waiting-rooms with natives. I detect an inconsistency in that argument, but think it best to say nothing for fear of a scene. Mr Varma looks as if he were up to anything. Mr Shams-ud-Deen has a gentler and more incisive mind. He is the only one worth talking to, but Mr Varma makes such a noise that it is impossible to say anything. On the whole it is an unsatisfactory interview, but when I leave they present me with several controversial pamphlets of their own composition. These tell me all they were trying to say. In fact, I find phrase after phrase occurring which I remembered in their conversation. Clearly they know their case by heart. Raymond finds me reading the pamphlets and remarks that he is all for the blacks, but Indians are more than he can stand; besides they spread jiggers and bubonic plague. Then he drives me out to Muthaiga. The windscreen of his car has been broken overnight, and the body heavily battered. He remarks that someone must have borrowed it.

Another Nairobi scene; an evening picnic in the game reserve from Government House. We consist of the Acting-Governor and his wife; the ADCs, an agricultural expert from England, and the Race Week house-party; the latter includes a whiskered cattle rancher, very tall and swarthy, in the clothes of a Mexican bandit; oddly enough he is called 'Boy'; his wife is slight and smart, with enormous eyes and an adventurous past; she once rode alone from Addis Ababa to Berbera; she, too, has a queer name – Genessie.

We drive to a place called Lone Tree, disturbing herds of zebra and wildebeeste; their eyes flash bright green, dazzled by our spotlight. We make a detour and see some hyenas – but not as close as the one at Harar – and little jumping creatures called dik-diks. Meanwhile, the servants have lit a great bonfire and put motor cushions round it. We sit down and eat supper, the ADCs doing all the polite drudgery that makes most picnics hideous; presently most of the party fall asleep, except poor Genessie, whom I keep awake with descriptions of Abyssinia (it is only some days later that I realise she knows far more about it than I do).

Already, in the few days I had spent at Nairobi, I found myself falling in love with Kenya. There is a quality about it which I have found nowhere else but in Ireland, of warm loveliness and breadth and generosity. It was not a matter of mere liking, as one likes any place where people are amusing and friendly and the climate is agreeable, but a feeling of personal tenderness. I think almost everyone in the highlands of Kenya has very much this feeling, more or less articulately. One hears them grumbling about trade conditions, about the local government and the home government, but one very rarely hears them abuse the country itself as one hears Englishmen abroad in any other part of the world. It is little to be wondered at if, when they feel their positions threatened, this feeling takes form in expressions of local patriotism which seem fantastic in Whitehall.

I am concerned in this book with first-hand impressions, and wish to avoid, as far as possible, raising issues which it is not in my scope to discuss at length, but personal experiences are dependent on general conditions and I cannot hope to make my emotions about Kenya intelligible unless I devote a few sentences to dissipating some of the humbug which has grown up about it.

One very common idea of Kenya is spread by such books as Frederic de Janzé's *Vertical Land*. I began this chapter with the description of a day spent in the de Janzé circle between Muthaiga and Torr's. My reason for doing so was first that it made a contrast with the churlish officialdom of the coast and secondly that, in point of fact, this happened to be the succession of events as I remember them, on my first day in Nairobi. People were insistent that I should not regard Race Week as typical of the life of the country, because 'the Happy Valley' has come in for too much notoriety in the past. No one reading a book about smart people in London or Paris takes them as representing the general life of the country; but it is exactly this inference which is drawn when a book is written about smart people in Kenya. Even in the set I met at Muthaiga, only a small number are quite so jolly all the year round. 'Boy', for instance, owns the largest cattle farm in the country and, incredible as it sounds, knows almost every beast individually by sight. Of the settler community in general, the great majority are far too busy on their farms to come to Nairobi, except on an occasional predatory exped- ition to the bank or the Board of Agriculture.

Another quite inconsistent line of criticism represents the settlers as a gang of rapacious adventurers. Mr Macgregor Ross's *Kenya from Within* did a great deal to popularise this view and, when the more sober London weeklies mention the affairs of East Africa, their comments are more often than not inspired by the same kind of mistaken highmindedness. It is, on the face of it, rather surprising to find a community of English squires established on the equator. By the doctrine, just old-fashioned enough to be prevalent in refined English circles, they have no business there at all; the soil is the inalienable property of the African coloured races, and the sooner it is made untenable for the white settlers, the better. This dogma, it may be noted, is not held to apply everywhere; its strongest advocates are quite ready to hasten the eviction of traditional landowners in their own country, while in the settlement of the Near East, two exercises in arbitrary statesmanship have been attempted which are in principle contradictory both to this attitude and to each other – the trans-shipment of Jews to Palestine and of Anatolian Christians to Greece.

But, of course, it is futile to attempt to impose any kind of theological consistency in politics, which are not an exact science but, by their nature, a series of makeshift, rule-of-thumb, practical devices for getting out of scrapes. There is in existence a body of serious opinion in England which holds that, in the past, the Africans have been unjustly exploited by European commercial interests, and is anxious to prevent this in future. It is unprofitable to discuss the question of abstract 'rights' to the land; if one does, one is led into all kinds of ethnological byways – have the Nilotic immigrant tribes any more 'right' in East Africa than the

British? One must confine oneself to recent history and rough justice. There is one general principle which one may accept; that the whole of history, from the earliest times until today, has been determined by the movements of peoples about the earth's surface; migratory tribes settled and adapted their cultures to new conditions; conquest, colonisation, commercial penetration, religious proselytising, topographical changes, land becoming worked out, pastures disappearing, harbours silting up – have preserved a constant fluidity of population. It is useless to pretend that, suddenly, at the beginning of the Boer War, the foundation of the Third International, or at this or that time in recent history, the piano stopped and the musical chairs were over, the lava stream cooled and congealed, and the whole process was at an end, for no other reason than that the enlightened people of Northern Europe – having lost their belief in revealed religion and falling back helplessly for moral guidance on their own tenderer feelings – have decided that it is Wrong. The process will go on, because it is an organic process in human life. One nation may artificially restrain its people from going to a certain place; it may bring about the ruin of those who do. But in the end the future of European settlement in Central Africa will depend on the suitability of the country for the foreign system of cultivation by large, individual landowners, on the ability of the immigrant races to maintain efficiency in an alien climate, to propagate there, and on the re-establishment of the world's markets on a basis which will enable them to sell their produce at a price high enough to maintain their standard of living. On first acquaintance, and for a few months' visit, the climate of the Kenya highlands is slightly intoxicating but wholly agreeable. It is still uncertain, however, whether Nordic people will be able to live permanently at that altitude and on that latitude. Until the second generation have grown up, it is impossible to say. Many of the children I met seemed perfectly normal in health, and peculiarly self-reliant; in others there seemed to be a somewhat morbid alternation of listlessness and high excitement. There is as yet no adequate secondary education. Those who can afford it, send their children to school in England.

It must be remembered that only a part – about two thousand families in all – of the small European population can be regarded as citizens of the colony. The officials and commercial agents serve their term and then retire to England; the settlers look upon the country as their permanent home; the two groups can scarcely be expected to regard local policy from the same point of view or with the same concern. The officials are sure of their pay and their pensions; the settlers mostly depend on local prosperity for their entire livelihood. They are people who bought their farms and sunk the whole of their capital in them; during the good years they re-invested the greater part of their profits in building, buying more land, machinery and stock. From many European accounts you might suppose that all they had done was to drive out a few scared natives and take possession of fully equipped properties, as though they were an invading army occupying an agricultural English county. Very large grants of land were made to early settlers, such as Lord Delamere, who had the means to develop them. Except in the case of pasturage the land was, as it stood, valueless for cultivation on a large scale; it consisted for the most part of tracts of bush country which had to be cleared either by hand or by machinery imported at great expense from abroad; there were no roads by which the products could be brought to market. It is, in fact, one of the many grounds for Indian complaint that the farmers have been obliged to undertake the task bit by bit, and that even now the greater part of the land distributed to Europeans is still waiting for full development. While the present uncertainty persists there is little inducement to the settlers to add to their commitments. Large fortunes have been made in the past by speculating in real estate at Mombasa and Nairobi. Throughout the country as a whole, however, investment in land – whether it has taken the form of clearing and planting free grants of virgin soil or of the actual purchase of already developed farmland – has, in the past ten years, proved barely profitable and during the last eighteen months, uniformly disastrous. It is not big business enterprise which induces the Kenya settlers to hang on to their houses and lands, but the more gentle motive of love for a very beautiful country that they have come to regard as their home, and the wish to transplant and perpetuate a habit of life traditional to them, which England has ceased to accommodate – the traditional life of the English squirearchy, which, while it was still dominant, formed the natural target for satirists of every shade of opinion, but to which now that it has become a rare and exotic survival, deprived of the normality which was one of its determining characteristics, we can as a race look back with unaffected esteem and regret. I am sure that, if any of them read this book, they will deny with some embarrassment this sentimental interpretation of their motives. It is part of the very vitality of their character that they should do so. They themselves will say simply that farming was impossible in England, so they came to Kenya, where they understood that things were better; they will then grouse a little about the government, and remark that after all, bad as things are, it is still possible to keep a horse or two and get excellent shooting – things only possible at home for those who spend the week in an office. That would be their way of saying what I have just said above. The Kenya settlers are not cranks of the kind who colonised New England, nor criminals and ne'er-do-wells of the kind who went to Australia, but perfectly normal, respectable Englishmen, out of sympathy with their own age, and for this reason linked to the artist in an unusual but very real way. One may regard them as quixotic in their attempt to re-create Barsetshire on the equator, but one cannot represent them as pirates and land-grabbers.

That particular charge, so often put forward by African Nationalists, would in any case apply directly only to a tiny section of the existing white population, the vast majority of whom came into the country after the question of inalienable native reserves had been, one hopes, finally settled. Even if grossest injustice had been done by the original settlers, it could hardly be expiated by a corresponding injustice to their successors. The question is not one of importance in the present situation. It may, however, be remarked that as a matter of fact there has never been an example of colonisation carried out with so little ill-will between the immigrant and the indigenous races, or with such scrupulous solicitude for the weaker party. At the time of the construction of the Uganda railway, vast tracts of the present colony of Kenya were completely uncultivated and uninhabited. Walls of desert were the only protection which the agricultural tribes could put up against the warrior tribes. It was from these neutral areas that a large proportion of the European farms were developed. In cases where natives were found in possession, they were asked to mark out the territory which they habitually used, allowance was made for their expansion and their whole area was made over to them before any claims by colonists were considered in the neighbourhood. That, at any rate, was the principle. It is impossible to say how far in practice there may have been corruption or mild coercion; whether the natives invariably understood that, in making their claims, they were limiting themselves permanently within the boundaries they drew out. It is, on the face of it, probable that in the general large process there were occasional failures to apply the principle in absolute purity; but there is no evidence that failure was at all extensive, except in the case of the Masai. No one can reasonably pretend that their treatment was just or expedient. It may be said, with perfect truth, that the Masai are a race of bullies; that the only international law they ever recognised was that of superior strength, and that they were treated according to their own morality. The fact remains that their wholesale eviction from Laikipia in 1904, where they had been induced to migrate with explicit guarantees of permanent possession, was gravely dishonourable according to European morality, and a blunder in statesmanship which was aggravated by the uncertainty with which it was carried out. The superb physique of the race fits them for the part of noble savage which nationalists have been eager enough to assign to them, and they remain the least responsive people in East Africa to the benevolent attentions of the Colonial Office. They have been prevented in their traditional pastime of murdering their pacific neighbours by the ingenious device of confiscating their shields (which thus

renders them and their herds defenceless against lion).
When, as compensation, they were offered the privilege of
participation in the late war, they refused, providing the only
example of wholly successful conscientious objection. Lately,
however, a new opening has been found for them as cinema
actors. Shields are dealt out – a restoration which, on one
occasion at least, resulted in a fine resumption of bloodshed – and they are sent out before a barrage of well-protected
cameramen to spear lion in the bush for the amusement of
European and American audiences, sheltering their court-
ships from the rain.

Everyone I met was anxious to impress on me that there
was no 'native problem'; that the whole thing was invented
in London and Bombay. It would be absurdly pretentious
after a few weeks in the country to make any general statement on a question as broad as that. What I can say with
conviction, however, is that all the European settlers I met,
while eschewing Colonial Office uplift, had a sense of
responsibility towards their native employees, and a half
humorous sympathy with them, which compared strikingly
with the attitude of most European capitalists towards fac-
tory hands. People abused their native servants in round
terms and occasionally cuffed their heads, as they did their
English servants up to the end of the eighteenth century.
The idea of courtesy to servants, in fact, only came into
being when the relationship ceased to be a human one and

became purely financial. The cases of cruelty of white to black, quoted by Mr Macgregor Ross, are mere examples of pathological criminality which can be found anywhere without distinction of race; white people are cruel to white, black to black, white to black, and when prestige is inoperative, black to white. The cases in *Kenya from Within* have some significance in their bearing on the way in which justice is administered in African courts, but none on the relationship of white masters to black servants. When the settlers say that there is no native problem, they mean that they can see nothing essentially incompatible between the welfare of the two races. I am sure that they are perfectly sincere in saying this. On the other hand they are alarmed by the Duke of Devonshire's term 'paramountcy'.[1]

I went to a pantomime in Nairobi, performed (incidentally extremely well) by amateurs. The comic man, dressed as the Widow Twankey or an ugly sister of Cinderella's, I forget which, had as one of his chief recurrent gags the line 'I will have paramountcy.' The word rankles and it is clearly embarrassing to the settlers that it should have been used by a Conservative Minister. If it had been coined by that most ridiculed nobleman, Lord Passfield of Passfield Corner, it could have been pigeon-holed as 'Labour' and forgotten;

1. Kenya White Paper 1923.

coming from the Duke of Devonshire it seems a betrayal of their cause in the quarter where they most expected support. There is a slight infection of persecution mania about all political thought in the colonies, just as there is megalomania in Europe. Words like 'paramountcy' are inflammatory. In its context the term is a typical assertion of public high-mindedness with no particular application. *'Primarily Kenya is an African territory and His Majesty's Government think it necessary definitely to record their considered opinion that the interests of the African natives must be paramount and that if, and when, those interests and the interests of the immigrant races should conflict, the former should prevail.'* There is very little menace in 'paramountcy', stated in this vaguely pious way. So far as the East African European interests are threatened by the policy declared in the White Paper of 1923, it seems to me to be in quite a sufficient direction; the insistence of the integrity of the territory as a whole introduces an essentially foreign bureaucratic attitude opposed to what is the present disposition of those on the spot to regard the white settled highlands and the native reserves as different states in a federation. There is no question of the white settlers being handed over to the rule of natives; there was a question of natives being ruled by settlers. There were serious objections to this and the object of the White Paper was to assert that the home government would not contemplate such a devolution of authority. A slightly sinister note, if one wishes to find one, lies in the ascription of the settled highlands to the 'primarily African' territory.

The relationship of settler to native is primarily that of an employer of labour, and there is no reason why this should not become easier rather than less easy as the second generation of natives grow up who are accustomed to the idea of white neighbours and curious to see more of the world than life in the reserves can offer. The fear apparent in the White Paper that officials are being used for semi-compulsory recruitment of labour, or that local taxation was assessed with the motive of driving natives outside the reserves to work, seems to have little foundation enough, and should, in the normal course of progress, rapidly disappear.

The Indian question, however, is a different matter. There was very nearly armed rebellion on the issue in 1923, and the ill feeling then aroused is still present, sometimes subterraneously complicating and embittering simple questions, often frankly apparent on both sides. The trouble is both social and political. The more educated, professional Indians resent their exclusion from the social life of the Europeans; they are not admitted to the hotels, bars or clubs of the colony and, in practice though not by law, they are segregated in railway trains and the residential quarters of towns. They are not allowed to occupy or speculate in land in the highlands. They outnumber the Europeans by rather more than two to one. In the allotment of non-official seats in the legislative council, provision is made for eleven elected Europeans and five elected Indians.[1] Education is kept separate between the races, each community being taxed at a different rate for the support of its own schools.[2] There is very little hope of high promotion for Indians in government service. There is a long list of 'grievances', which Mr Varma spat out at me as though I were individually responsible for them all; until, in fact, I began to wish that I were. He resented the fact that separate lavatories were provided for Indians in trains; he said that, as a member of the British Empire, he insisted on owning land in the highlands. I asked whether he set great store by his membership of the Empire and he said he did not. I asked him whether the cultivation of a highland farm would not interfere with his practice in Nairobi. For reply he quoted figures that seemed to show that an Indian who owned a farm near the Nandi escarpment had done better with his coffee than his European neighbours. When, later, I asked his European neighbours they said that the farm was notorious for miles round as the breeding-place of every pest which afflicted their crops. It is impossible to find out the truth when you really get down to the brass tacks of racial

1. Also for one Arab and one missionary nominated to represent native interests.
2. There is also a liquor tax devoted to education, divided proportionately between the two communities.

antagonism. Most of the 'grievances' involved no particular hardship, except deprivation of European intercourse, for which it is hard to believe Mr Varma had any sincere aspiration.

The situation is that the settlers want Kenya to consist of white people, owning the soil and governing themselves, and Indians to be foreigners, allowed full freedom of trade but divorced from the life of the country; the Indians want it to be an Indian colony governed on the wretched old principle of head-counting, which they have pulled out of the pie of European education. Both sides are capable of hypocrisy in their bandying about of the phrase 'native welfare' to support their claims. I do not think that the most whole-hearted supporter of Indian Nationalism would claim that the East African Indians were suitable 'trustees' for a 'people not yet able to stand by themselves under the strenuous conditions of the modern world',[1] nor, I think, would Major Grogan maintain that the majority of settlers came to Kenya primarily to protect the pagans from Hindu influence.

At the time of writing, the situation, complicated by the commission on closer Union, is in an impasse. The Indians refuse to take up the seats allotted them in the council; the business of government is managed by the official Europeans and criticised by the elected ones. The Indians hold out for a

1. Kenya White Paper.

common electoral roll; the Hilton Young Commission – whose whole report was an example of the futility of the attempt to scrutinise evidence by a body who were not previously agreed upon their political principles – advised a common franchise, if adopted with the consent of the European community. It is probable that Mr Varma would refuse his common franchise if it came to him with European consent, and it is quite certain that European consent will not be forthcoming. Meanwhile, no one finds the lack of Indian cooperation a serious embarrassment, except the Government of India, who have been at greater difficulty in persuading Indians in India of the essentially harmonious natures of the two races, and of the advantages accruing to membership of the British Empire, while events are following this course in East Africa.

It is barely possible to explain to North Europeans the reality of race antagonism. For so many generations the Mediterranean peoples have been at war with the infidel that they have learned to accept it calmly as a normal thing, and therefore seem often to be immune from it, as Turks are said at advanced age to become immune from syphilis. But the Northern races, confronted with the danger of domination or infection by a coloured race, tend to go a little mad on the subject. The fear of Indians, Negroes, Japanese or Chinese obsesses one or other of all the branches of the Nordic race who, by leaving their own sea mists and twilight, have exposed themselves to these strangers. Anglo-Saxons are perhaps worse than any. It is easy enough for Anglo-Saxons in London, whose only contact with coloured peoples is to hear gramophone records of spirituals, or occasionally share a 'bus with a polite, brown student, to be reasonable about the matter and laugh at the snobbery of their cousins in India or shudder at the atrocities of their more distant cousins in Virginia, but the moment they put on a topi, their sanity gently oozes away. 'You can see *he* hasn't been out before,' someone remarked to me in an outward-bound liner as we observed an Englishman offering some mild, normal courtesy to a negro first-class passenger. Alas, it was true. In East Africa as yet there are no negroes in positions where they could possibly contemplate equality with the whites; Anglo-Saxon sanity remains undisturbed in that direction. But when some newly arrived Anglo-Saxon advises equal franchise with Indians (on a basis of qualification by education which will still enable the Anglo-Saxon to keep dominance in practice though resigning it in theory), then there is a talk about kidnapping the Governor and the 'Boston tea-party'. It is not a matter one can be censorious about. Gentle reader, you would behave in just the same way yourself after a year in the tropics. It is just a lack of reasoning – I will not call it a failing – to which our race is prone as the Malays are prone to periodical fits of homicidal mania. The reciprocal feeling which people like Mr Varma have about Anglo-Saxons is every bit as unbalanced. It really is not a thing to censure, but it is something to be remembered when considering the temperament of this equatorial Barsetshire. And one other point – it is just conceivable that they might be right. When over a long period a great number of otherwise respectable people consistently deny the conclusions of their own reason on some particular point, it may be a disease like roulette, or it may be a revelation like the miracles of Lourdes. It is just worth considering the possibility that there may be something valuable behind the indefensible and inexplicable assumption of superiority by the Anglo-Saxon race.

As I have said above, it is uncertain whether the kind of life which the Kenya settlers are attempting to re-establish is capable of survival; whether there may not be in the next twenty-five years a general Withdrawal of the Legions to defend Western civilisation at its sources. But, whatever its future, it is an experiment in transplanted social institutions as interesting in its way as the Spanish settlement of America or the Norman baronies of the Levant.

At the end of Race Week, Raymond and I left Nairobi and drove through the Rift Valley to Lake Naivasha. A bad road; red earth cut into deep ruts; one of the best roads in the country. On the way we pass other settlers returning to their farms; they wear bright shirts and wide felt hats; they drive box-body cars, in most cases heaped with miscellaneous hardware they have been buying at the capital; groups of

Kikuyu, the women with heavy luggage on their backs supported by a strap round their foreheads; their ears are slit and ornamented; their clothes of copper-coloured skins; the men have mostly made some effort at European dress in the form of discarded khaki shorts or an old hat. They attempt a clumsy kind of salute as we pass, smiling and saying 'Jambo bwana', rather as children in England still wave their pocket handkerchiefs to trains. I have heard it said that you can tell the moment you cross into Kenya from Uganda or Tanganyika territory by the sulky, oppressed demeanour of the natives. That seemed to me true, later, of the South African Union but without foundation in Kenya. Perhaps the observation was first made by someone crossing from the south directly into the Masai reserve; anyway, journalists in London have found it a convenient remark to repeat.

The scenery is tremendous, finer than anything I saw in Abyssinia; all round for immense distances successive crests of highland. In England we call it a good view if we can see a church spire across six fields; the phrase, made comic by the Frankaus of magazine fiction, 'Wide Open Spaces', really does mean something here. Brilliant sunshine quite unobscured, uninterrupted in its incidence; sunlight clearer than daylight; there is something of the moon about it, the coolness seems so unsuitable. Amber sunlight in Europe; diamond sunlight in Africa. The air fresh as an advertisement for toothpaste.

We are going to stay with Kiki. She lives in a single-storeyed, very luxurious house on the edge of the lake. She came to Kenya for a short Christmas visit. Someone asked her why she did not stay longer. She explained that she had nowhere particular to go. So he gave her two or three miles of lake front for a Christmas present. She has lived there off and on ever since. She has a husband who shoots most sorts of animals, and a billiard-room to accommodate their heads. She also has two children and a monkey, which sleeps on her pillow. There was an English general staying in the house. He had come all the way from England to shoot a rare animal called a bongo; he had meant to spend all the winter that way. He got his bongo the first week on safari. He felt rather at a loose end. The General was delightful. One day after dinner we talked about marriage and found ourselves in agreement on the subject. (A little while ago I was lunching at a restaurant in London when I was suddenly hit hard between the shoulders and someone said 'Jambo bwana'. It was the General. I asked him to luncheon next week, and secured numerous beautiful girls to talk to him. He never came.)

It was lovely at Naivasha; the grass ran down from the house to the water, where there was a bathing-place with a little jetty to take one clear of the rushes. We used to swim in the morning, eat huge luncheons and sleep in the after- noon. Kiki appeared soon after tea. There were small, hot sausages at cocktail time. Often, very late after dinner, we went into the kitchen and cooked eggs. (There is an important division between the sort of house where you are allowed to cook after midnight, and the house where, if you are hungry, dry sandwiches are shown you, between decanters.) Once Kiki and I went for a walk as far as some ants, fifty yards up the garden. She said, 'You must just feel how they can sting,' and lifted a very large one on to the back of my hand with a leaf. It stung frightfully. More than that, several others ran up the leg of my trouser and began stinging there.

In Kenya it is easy to forget that one is in Africa; then one is reminded of it suddenly, and the awakening is agreeable. One day before luncheon we were sitting on the terrace with cocktails. Kiki's husband and the General were discussing someone they had blackballed for White's; Raymond was teaching chemin-de-fer to Kiki's little boy; there was a striped awning over our heads and a gramophone – all very much like the South of France. Suddenly a Kikuyu woman came lolloping over the lawn, leading a little boy by the hand. She said she wanted a pill for her son. She explained the sort of pain he had. Kiki's husband called his valet and translated the explanation of the pain. The valet advised soda mint. When he brought it, the woman held out her hand but they – to the woman's obvious displeasure – insisted on giving it directly to the child. 'Otherwise she would eat it herself the moment she was round the corner.' Apparently the Kikuyu have a passion for pills only equalled in English Bohemia; they come at all hours to beg for them, usually on the grounds that their children are ill, just as Europeans beg for sixpences.

After a time Kiki made a sudden appearance before breakfast, wearing jodhpurs and carrying two heavy bore guns. She had decided to go and kill some lions.

So Raymond and I went to his house at Njoro.

One does not – or at any rate I did not – look upon farming as the occupation of a bachelor, perhaps only because I had so often seen the words 'Farmer's Wife' staring at me from hoardings or perhaps through some atavistic feeling of sympathetic magic that fertility in promoting crops and family were much the same thing. Whatever the reason, the large number of bachelor farmers was, to me, one of the surprising things about Kenya. Raymond is one, though perhaps he is more typically bachelor than farmer. I spent about a fortnight with him off and on at Njoro; sometimes he was away for a day or two, sometimes I was. A delightful if rather irregular visit. His cook was away all the time. There was a head boy called Dunston who spent most of the day squatting outside cooking bath water on a wood fire. I learned very few words of Swahili. When I woke up I said, 'Woppe chickule, Dunston?' which meant, 'Where is food, Dunston?' Dunston usually replied, 'Hapana chickule bwana,' which meant, 'No food, my lord.' Sometimes I had no breakfast; sometimes I found Raymond, if he was at home, sitting up in bed with a tin of grouse paste and a bottle of soda-water, and forced him to share these things with me; sometimes if the telephone was working I rang up Mrs Grant, the nearest neighbour, and had breakfast with her. We used to lunch and dine at the Njoro golf club or with the neighbours: very friendly dinner-parties, Irish in character, to which we bounced over miles of cart-track in a motor van which Raymond had just acquired in exchange for his car; it was full of gadgets designed to help him capture gorillas in the Eturi forest – a new idea of Raymond's, prompted by the information that they fetched two thousand pounds a head at the Berlin Zoo – but was less comfortable than the car for ordinary social use.

The houses of Kenya are mainly in that style of architecture which derives from intermittent prosperity. In many of them the living-rooms are in separate buildings from the bedrooms; their plan is usually complicated by a system of additions and annexes which have sprung up in past years as the result of a good crop, a sudden burst of optimism, the influx of guests from England, the birth of children, the arrival of pupil farmers, or any of the many chances of domestic life. In many houses there is sadder evidence of building begun and abandoned when the bad times came on. Inside they are, as a rule, surprisingly comfortable. Up an unfenced cart-track, one approaches a shed made of concrete, match-boarding, and corrugated iron, and, on entering, finds oneself among old furniture, books, and framed miniatures.

There are very few gardens; we went to one a few miles

outside Njoro where an exquisite hostess in golden slippers led us down grass paths bordered with clipped box, over Japanese bridges, pools of water-lilies and towering tropical plants. But few settlers have time for these luxuries.

Boy and Genessie, with whom I spent a week-end, have one of the 'stately homes' of Kenya; three massive stone buildings on the crest of a hill at Elmenteita overlooking Lake Nakuru, in the centre of an estate which includes almost every topographical feature – grass, bush forest, rock, river, waterfall, and a volcanic cleft down which we scrambled on the end of a rope.

On the borders a bush fire is raging, a low-lying cloud by day, at night a red glow along the horizon. The fire dominates the week-end. We watch anxiously for any change in the wind; cars are continually going out to report progress; extra labour is mustered and dispatched to 'burn a brake'; will the flames 'jump' the railroad? The pasture of hundreds of head of cattle is threatened.

In the evening we go down to the lakeside to shoot duck; thousands of flamingo lie on the water; at the first shot they rise in a cloud, like dust from a beaten carpet; they are the colour of pink alabaster; they wheel round and settle further out. The head of a hippopotamus emerges a hundred yards from shore and yawns at us. When it is dark the hippo comes out for his evening walk. We sit very still, huddled along the running-boards of the cars. We can hear heavy footsteps and the water dripping off him; then he scratches himself noisily. We turn the spotlight of the car on him and reveal a great mud-caked body and a pair of resentful little pink eyes; then he trots back into the water.

Again the enchanting contradictions of Kenya life; a baronial hall straight from Queen Victoria's Scottish Highlands – an open fire of logs and peat with carved-stone chimney-piece, heads of game, the portraits of prize cattle, guns, golf-clubs, fishing-tackle, and folded newspapers – sherry is brought in, but, instead of a waistcoated British footman, a bare-footed Kikuyu boy in white gown and red jacket. A typical English meadow of deep grass; model cow-sheds in the background; a pedigree Ayrshire bull scratching his back on the gatepost; but, instead of rabbits, a company of monkeys scutter away at our approach; and, instead of a smocked yokel, a Masai herdsman draped in a blanket, his hair plaited into a dozen dyed pig-tails.

I returned to Njoro to find Raymond deeply involved in preparations for his gorilla hunt; guns, cameras, telescopes, revolvers, tinned food, and medicine chests littered tables and floors. There was also a case of champagne. 'You have to have that to give to Belgian officials – and, anyway, it's always useful.'

That evening I dined with the Grants. They had an Englishwoman staying with them whose daughter had been in the party at Genessie's. She was a prominent feminist, devoted to the fomentation of birth-control and regional cookery in rural England, but the atmosphere of Kenya had softened these severe foibles a little; she was anxious not to be eaten by a lion. It had been arranged that we should all climb Mount Kilimanjaro together; this plan, however, was modified, and, instead, we decided to go to Uganda. I wanted to visit Kisumu before leaving Kenya, so it was decided that they should pick me up there on the following Sunday. Next day I watched Raymond loading his van, and that evening we had a heavy evening at the Njoro club. Early the day after, I took the train for Kisumu.

It was here that I had one of the encounters that compensate one for the blank, nightmare patches of travelling. I was going second class. My companion in the carriage was a ginger-haired young man a few years older than myself; he had an acquaintance with whom he discussed technicalities of local legislation; later this man got out and we were left alone. For some time we did not speak to each other. It was a tedious journey. I tried to read a copy of Burton's *Anatomy of Melancholy* which I had stolen from Raymond's shelves. Presently he said, 'Going far?'

'Kisumu.'

'What on earth for?'

'No particular reason. I thought I might like it.'

Pause. 'You're new in the country, aren't you?'

'Yes.'

'I thought you must be. Kisumu's bloody.'

Presently he said again: 'What have you seen so far?'

I told him briefly.

'Yes, that's all most visitors see. They're delightful people, mind you, but they aren't typical of Kenya.'

Two or three stations went by without any further con-versation. Then he began getting together his luggage – a kit bag, some baskets, a small packing-case, and an iron stove-pipe. 'Look here. You won't like Kisumu. You'd far better stay with me the night.'

'All right.'

'Good.'

We got out at a station near the Nandi escarpment and transferred his luggage to a Ford van that was waiting some distance away in charge of an Indian shopkeeper.

'I hope you don't mind; I've got to see my brother-in-law first. It isn't more than thirty miles out of the way.'

We drove a great distance along a rough track through country of supreme beauty. At crossroads the signposts simply bore the names of the settlers. Eventually we arrived at the house. There were several people there, among them a man I had been at school with. Until then my host and I did not know each other's names. There was an Italian garden, with trimmed yew hedges and grass, balustraded terrace, and a vista of cypresses; in the distance the noble horizon of the Nandi hills; after sundown these came alight with little points of fire from the native villages; the household

was playing poker under a thatched shelter. My host trans-
acted his business; we drank a glass of Bristol Cream and
continued the journey. It was now quite dark. Another very
long drive. At last we reached our destination. A boy came
out to greet us with a lantern, followed by an elderly lady –
my host's mother-in-law. 'I thought you were dead,' she said.
'And who is this?'

'He's come to stay. I've forgotten his name.'

'You'll be very comfortable; there's nothing in the home
to eat and there are three swarms of bees in the dining-room.'
Then, turning to her son-in-law: 'Belinda's hind-quarters are
totally paralysed.'

This referred, not, as I assumed, to her daughter, but, I
learned later, to a wolfhound bitch.

We went up to the house – a spacious, single-storeyed
building typical of the colony. I made some polite comment
on it.

'Glad you like it. I built most of it myself.'

'It is the third we have had in this spot,' remarked the old
lady. 'The other two were destroyed. The first caught fire; the
second was struck by lightning. All the furniture I brought
out from England was demolished. I have had dinner prepared three nights running. Now there is nothing.'

There was, however, an excellent dinner waiting for us
after we had had baths and changed into pyjamas. We spent
the evening dealing with the bees, who, at nightfall, had dis-

posed themselves for sleep in various drawers and cupboards about the living-room. They lay in glutinous, fermenting masses, crawling over each other, like rotten cheese under the microscope; a fair number flew about the room stinging us as we dined; while a few abandoned outposts lurked among the embroidered linen sheets in the bedrooms. A subdued humming filled the entire house. Baths of boiling water were brought in, and the torpid insects were shovelled into them by a terrified native boy. Some of the furniture was carried out on to the lawn to await our attention in the morning.

Next day we walked round the farm – a coffee plantation. Later, a surveyor of roads arrived and we drove all over the countryside pointing out defective culverts. During the rains, the old lady told me, the farm was sometimes isolated from its neighbours for weeks at a time. We saw a bridge being built under the supervision, apparently, of a single small boy in gumboots. Poor Belinda lay in a basket on the verandah, while over her head a grey and crimson parrot heartlessly imitated her groans.

The surveyor took me to the station for the afternoon train to Kisumu – a town which proved as dreary as my host had predicted – numerous brand-new, nondescript houses, a small landing-stage and railway junction, a population entirely Indian or official. The hotel was full; I shared a bedroom with an Irish airman who was prospecting for the

Imperial Airways route to the Cape. Next day, Sunday, I went to church and heard a rousing denunciation of birth-control by a young Mill Hill Father. The manager of the hotel took me for a drive in his car to a Kavirondo village where the people still wore no clothes except discarded Homburg hats. Then Mrs Grant arrived with the feminist and her daughter.

We drove to Eldoret and stayed at one more house, the most English I had yet seen – old silver, family portraits, chintz-frilled dressing-tables – and next day crossed the frontier into Uganda.

Four

In its whole character, Uganda is quite distinct from Kenya. It is a protectorate not a colony. Instead of the estates of white settlers, one finds evidence of European interest, in seminaries, secondary schools, 'homes', welfare centres, Christian missions of all denominations, theological colleges, and innumerable frantic cyclists.

Long before the coming of Arabs or English, the Baganda people had attained a fair degree of organisation. They had, and still have, a centralised monarchy, an hereditary aristocracy, a complex and consistent system of law. They are quick-witted – so much so that Sir Harry Johnston had described them as 'the Japanese of Africa' – and ambitious of education. They have accepted Christianity, some as a mere constituent part of the glamorous Western civilisation they covet, others with genuine spiritual fervour. They have thrown themselves eagerly into theological controversy, hurtling texts backwards and forwards like shuttlecocks; there are several magazines in Kampala, edited and written by natives, devoted almost exclusively to this form of journalism. They take a lively interest in the technicalities and theories of local government, land tenure, and trade organ-isation. The national costume is a model of decency – a single white gown which covers them completely to neck, wrist, and ankle. They have a written language which can boast a literature of sorts; in addition to which many of them speak both English and Swahili.

Of course, this culture is remarkable only in comparison with their savage neighbours in Kenya, Tanganyika, and the Congo, and it is confined to a minority among the Baganda. The population of the Protectorate is still for the most part made up of completely unsophisticated peasant cultivators. The inhabitants of an ordinary Baganda village do not show evidence of any special superiority; they do differ radically, however, from their neighbours in having a conscious national unity and a progressive intelligentsia. They are being educated towards the old-fashioned ideal of representative institutions, and official British policy abhors the idea of a permanent white population which might embarrass this development, as it will do in Kenya.

There was nothing, however, to mark the frontiers of the two territories. We crossed sometime during the morning and arrived at Jinja in the late afternoon. It would be tedious to describe each of the lakeside settlements; they vary in size, but are all identical in character, neat, sanitary, straggling; a landing-stage and an office; sometimes a railway station and an hotel; sometimes a golf links; genial, official nonentities, punctilious and slightly patronising. Entebbe is drearier than most; Jinja slightly gayer; Kisumu is the norm.

At Jinja there is both hotel and golf links. The latter is, I believe, the only course in the world which posts a special rule that the player may remove his ball by hand from hippopotamus footprints. For there is a very old hippopotamus who inhabits this corner of the lake. Long before the dedication of the Ripon Falls it was his practice to take an evening stroll over that part of the bank which now constitutes the town of Jinja. He has remained set in his habit, despite railway-lines and bungalows. At first, attempts were made to shoot him, but lately he has come to be regarded as a local mascot, and people returning late from bridge parties not infrequently see him lurching home down the main street. Now and then he varies his walk by a detour across the golf links and it is then that the local rule is brought into force.

There were several big-game hunters staying in the hotel, so that there was not room for all of us. Accordingly I went off to the Government rest-house. These exist all over Africa, primarily for the convenience of travelling officials, but private individuals may make use of them, if they are empty. They vary in range from small hotels to unfurnished shelters. At Jinja there was a bedstead and mattress, but no sheets or blankets. I had just made a collection of the overcoats of the party when we saw a black face grinning at us from below the hotel steps. It was Dunston, hat in hand, come to report the loss of Raymond. He and the neighbour who was joining his gorilla hunt had gone on in a car, leaving Dunston and the native driver to follow in the van. Somewhere they had missed the road. Anyway, here was the van with the rifles and provisions and 'Hapana bwana de Trafford'. Dunston wanted instructions. We told him to take bwana de Trafford's blankets to the rest-house, make up the bed, and then wait for further instructions. Meanwhile we wired to Eldoret, Njoro, and Nairobi, reporting the position of Raymond's lorry. I do not know whether he ever found it, for we left next morning for Kampala.

Here I said good-bye to my companions and established myself at the hotel. I was becoming conscious of an inclin- ation to return to Europe and wanted to get down to Albertville and the Belgian air service as soon as I could. A kind-hearted young travel agent tried to persuade me to pay him £60 to arrange my route through Lake Kivu, but I found in the end that it would be quicker and a great deal cheaper to stick to the regular service round Lake Victoria to Mwanza; from there to Tabora and Kigoma, and so across Lake Tan- ganyika to my goal. From now on, this record becomes literally a 'travel book'; that is to say that it deals less with the observation of places than with the difficulties of getting from one place to another.

There were still five days, however, to put in before the lake steamer called for Mwanza, and these days I spent in a milieu that was mainly ecclesiastical, for the missions hold most of the strings of Uganda policy.

In reaction from the proselytising fervour of fifty years ago, there is at the moment a good deal of distrust of foreign missions. Many officials, in unofficial moments, will confess that if they had their way they would like to clear all the missionaries out of the country; many private persons told me that they would never engage a 'mission boy' as a servant – they were always dishonest and often insolent. By an anti-imperialist interpretation of history, missionaries are regarded as the vanguard of commercial penetration. Romantics with a taste for local colour denounce them as the spoil-sports who have clothed the naked and displaced fine native carving with plaster statuettes of the Sacred Heart. More serious sociologists maintain that tribal integrity, and with it the whole traditional structure of justice and morality, is being undermined by the suppression of tribal initiation ceremonies. Many good churchmen in Europe are not, I think, free from a slight resentment at the large sums yearly subscribed and dispatched for the doubtful benefit of remote corners of the globe, which might be employed at home on work of immediate and obvious importance. From all sides, criticism is being directed against these heroic outposts. One cannot remain a night in Kampala without finding one's sympathies involved on one side or the other.

Of course, from the theological aspect, there is no room

for doubt; every soul baptised, educated in the Faith and upheld by the sacraments in Christian life, whether it inhabits a black or white body, is so much positive good. Moreover, since growth is a measure of life, it is impossible that the Faith should not spread – expansion is organically inseparable from its existence. But theological arguments have little efficacy in modern controversy. It seems to me that this can be conceded to the general scepticism about Westernisation: that had it been possible to prevent alien influence – European, Arab, or Indian – from ever penetrating into Africa; could the people have lived in invincible ignorance, developing their own faith and institutions from their own roots; then, knowing what a mess we have made of civilisation in Europe and the immense compensating ills that attend every good we have accomplished, we may say that it would have been a mischievous thing, as long as there were any pagans left in Europe, to try and convert Africa. But it is quite certain that, in the expansive optimism of the last century, Africa would not have been left alone. Whether it wanted or not, it was going to be heaped with all the rubbish of our own continent; mechanised transport, representative government, organised labour, artificially stimulated appetites for variety in clothes, food, and amusement were waiting for the African round the corner. All the negative things were coming to him inevitably. Europe has only one positive thing which it can offer to anyone, and that is what the missionaries brought. In Uganda the missionaries got there before the trader or the official, and it is to this priority that they owe their unique position as managers of the entire elementary and secondary education of a country in which education is regarded as the highest function of government.

Kampala is built on seven hills, three of which are occupied by ecclesiastical buildings. There is the great cathedral at Ruaga, the Mill Hill mission at Nsambia, and, opposite them, the Church Missionary Society's cathedral – a really beautiful domed building, made entirely by native workmen. On a fourth is Makerere College, a secular institution, where the prize students of the mission schools receive a fairly advanced education. It is hoped that eventually this will form the nucleus of an East African university. Meanwhile the entrance examinations are hotly contested. Rivalry is intense between the Catholic missions and the CMS. It is not forty years since the last religious war was fought there. The occasional lapses into polygamy of the native Protestant clergy are greeted by the Catholic laity with unchristian delight, and the Makerere class lists are watched as a fair indication of the relative merits of the two faiths.

At the time of the religious war the issues had become fatally confused with the question of nationality. Today the Catholic missions have become thoroughly cosmopolitan; at Ruaga they are mainly French, but Bishop Camplin at Nsambia is a Scotsman, Mother Kevin at Kokonjiro is Irish, the

Teaching Brothers are, many of them, Canadian, and Father Janssen, the parish priest of Kampala, is Dutch. It was Father Janssen who acted as my guide during the five days at Kampala; an unforgettable figure, with vast beard, gaitered legs, and pipe of foul Boer tobacco, who drove about the town on a motor-bicycle defending the purity of his converts, when necessary, by force. He had built most of his church with his own hands, making clever counterfeits of wood-carving with the aid of a cement-mould and a paint-pot. With him I went round fever wards, maternity homes, schools, and seminaries; a gallant, indefatigable, inflexible man. His only personal ambition was to get away from the smug amenities of Kampala into the wilds, preferably to the head-hunters of Borneo, where he had begun his service.

We went out together to luncheon at Kokonjiro, a convent of native girls presided over by two European nuns and a woman doctor. They wear habit and live by strict rule; here they are trained as nurses and school teachers. At the convent they manage a small farm and hospital, and in recreation time do skilled needlework. It does not sound very remarkable to a reader in Europe; it is astounding in Central Africa – this little island of order and sweetness in an ocean of rank barbarity; all round it for hundreds of miles lies gross jungle, bush and forest, haunted by devils and the fear of darkness, where human life merges into the cruel, automatic life of the animals; here they were singing the offices just as they had been sung in Europe when the missions were little radiant points of learning and decency in a pagan wilderness. The only thing which upset the calm of Kokonjiro was the ravages of white ants in the sanctuary steps.

On the way back we stopped at a boys' school kept by Teaching Brothers; a loutish class were at work on the history syllabus of Makerere. The subject that afternoon was 'The Rivalry between Venice and Genoa in the Sixteenth Century'. Professor Huxley, in *African View*, derided the teaching of Latin at the Tabora seminary. It seems to me that the Makerere history syllabus is a far more notable example of unimaginative education. Swahili, his local dialect, and the kind of colloquial English he is likely to learn in the secular schools do not give the African a vehicle he can use with precision when his mind comes to interest itself in the more complex aspects of his own existence; Latin, intrinsically, is of value to him. But what sort of significance can the details of European history have to a man who will most probably never leave his own territory, and has never seen more than a handful of Europeans in his life?

I left Kampala on the following Sunday afternoon. The *Rusinga*, in which I travelled down the lake, was a comfortable little boat staffed with four smart officers who wore white and gold uniforms in the mornings and blue and gold at night. The voyage was uneventful; at Entebbe we ran into a plague of small fly; an Indian clerk in new boots paced the deck all night and kept me awake. On Tuesday we reached Bukoba and took on several more passengers; for the first time we came under grey skies, a pleasant experience after the invariable white glare of the preceding months. From now on we were in the rains. Bukoba was German built, before the war. It has rather more character than the other lake stations, with acacia avenues and substantial little houses with sturdy porticoes. On Wednesday I disembarked at Mwanza, where I spent a day and a half in a grubby hotel kept by a Greek. It is a deadly little town populated chiefly by Indians. I had to share a room with a CMS chaplain. At meals I sat with him and an elderly 'tough-egg' from Manchester, engaged in the cotton trade. At least he was so engaged until Thursday morning. He had come down from the south to meet his local manager. When he returned from the interview I asked, with what I hoped would be acceptable jocularity, 'Well, did you get the sack?'

'Yes,' he answered, 'as a matter of fact, I did. How the devil did you know?'

An unfortunate episode.

Later at luncheon he got rather drunk and told some very unsuitable anecdotes about a baboon. The missionary went off immediately to write letters in the bedroom. That evening we took the train to Tabora and arrived at noon next day. I travelled with the missionary, a cultured and courteous man. We talked about the language problem. A conference was sitting at that time, and had just decided to make Kiswahili compulsory throughout the three territories of Kenya, Uganda, and Tanganyika. On the whole, local opinion seems to favour this policy, though at first sight there seems little to commend it except the consideration that all the officials have learned the language at some pains and do not want to see their industry wasted. It is clearly desirable that there should be a *lingua franca*. Most of the local dialects are quite inadequate for educated employment. There is, for example, no word in Kikuyu for 'virgin' and no stage of Kikuyu womanhood with which any parallel to it can be drawn. This, as may be imagined, has caused considerable difficulty to missionaries. My travelling companion's point was that it was essential that Africans should speak a language of African origin; this seemed unduly doctrinaire. The same policy was defended to me on other grounds by the editor of a local newspaper, who maintained that it tended to preserve race superiority if English remained occult.

We also discussed the rite of female circumcision, which is one of the battlegrounds between missionaries and anthropologists. The missionary told me of an interesting experiment that was being made in his district. 'We found it impossible to eradicate the practice,' he said, 'but we have cleansed it of most of its objectionable features. The operation is now performed by my wife, in the wholesome atmosphere of the church hut.'

Perhaps it is by arrangement with the hotel proprietors that every change of train involves the delay of a night or two. It was not until late on Sunday evening that I could get my connection to Kigoma. Even in Africa the hotel at Tabora is outstandingly desolate. It is very large and old. In the optimistic days of German imperialism it was built to provide the amusement of an important garrison. It is now rapidly falling to pieces under the management of a dispirited Greek. One enters from the terrace into a large, double ballroom from which open a dining-room and a bar; music-stands and a broken drum lie on a dais at one end. In the centre is a threadbare billiard table. The bedrooms are in a wing; they open into a cool arcaded corridor; each is provided with a balcony and a bath-room. The paint had long ago worn off the bath; the tap would neither turn on or off, but dripped noisily day and night; the balcony had been used as a repository for derelict chairs; two panes of glass in the windows had been broken and stuffed with rag. My only companion here was a commercial traveller in cigarettes. We spent a long afternoon together playing poker-dice for shilling points. At the end of the day we were all square.

The town is not without interest. It reflects the various stages of its history. Fine groves of mango remain to record the days of Arab occupation, when it was the principal clearing station for slaves and ivory on the caravan route to the coast. Acacia-trees, a fort, and that sad hotel remain from the days of German East Africa. It was for some time the base of von Letow's gallant campaign; it was here that he coined his own gold – the Tabora sovereign much coveted by collectors. England's chief contribution is a large public school for the education of the sons of chiefs. This institution, erected at vast expense as a sop to the League of Nations, from which we hold the mandate, is one of the standing jokes of East Africa. Bishop Michaud, who very kindly called on me and drove me about in his car, took me to inspect it. It is a huge concrete building of two storeyes, planted prominently on one of the most unsuitable sites in the territory for the agricultural demonstrations that are the principal feature of its training. At first it was intended exclusively for future chiefs, but now it has been opened to other promising natives. They wear crested blazers and little rugger caps; they have prefects and 'colours'; they have a brass band; they learn farming, typewriting, English, physical drill, and public-school *esprit de corps*. They have honour boards, on which the name of one boy is inscribed every year. Since there were no particular honours for which they could compete – Makerere was far above their wildest ambitions – it was originally the practice of the boys to elect their champion. Elections, however, proved so unaccountably capricious that nomination soon took their place. I was invited to attend a *shari* (the local word for any kind of discussion). This was a meeting of the whole school, at which the prefects dealt with any misdemeanours.

They sat in chairs on a dais; the school squatted on the floor of the great hall. Three boys were called up: two had smoked; one had refused to plough. They were sentenced to be caned. Resisting strongly, they were pinioned to the ground by their friends while the drill-sergeant, an old soldier from the KAR, delivered two or three strokes with a cane. It was a far lighter punishment than any at an English public school, but it had the effect of inducing yells of agony and the most extravagant writhings. Apparently this part of the public-school system had not been fully assimilated.

We drove out to the ruins of the Arab house where Stanley and Livingstone had spent three weeks together. On the way we passed the residence of a local chief whose history illustrates the difference between English and African ideas of justice. A few months before my arrival he had been arrested for very considerable defalcations of public accounts. There was not the smallest doubt of his guilt in anyone's mind. He was sent down to the coast for trial, and there acquitted upon some purely technical legal quibble. To the European this seemed an excellent example of British impartiality; anyone, black or white, guilty or not guilty, got a fair trial according to law on the evidence submitted. To the native there was only one explanation; he had bribed or intimidated his judges. Under German administration, justice was often ruthless, but it was delivered arbitrarily by the officer on the spot, and the sentence executed immediately in a way that the natives understood; English justice, more tender and sophisticated, with its rights of appeal and delays of action, is more often than not confusing and unsatisfactory to the African mind.

That evening an opinionated little Austrian sisal-farmer arrived at the hotel, full of ridicule of British administration. He had just returned to the farm he had worked before the war, as Germans and Austrians are now doing in large numbers. He was confident that after a few more years of British mismanagement the territory would have to be handed back to Germany. 'Before the war,' he said, 'every native had to salute every European or he knew the reason why. Now, with all this education . . .' He was as boring as any retired colonel in an English farce.

On Saturday evening the cigarette traveller and I went to an Indian cinema. We saw a very old Charlie Chaplin film, made long before his rise to eminence, but full of all the tricks that have now become world famous; there was even an unhappy ending – his renunciation of love in favour of the handsome bounder. There was also a scene which was clearly the first version of the exquisite passage in *Gold Rush* where he eats the old boot; he is sitting under a tree, about to begin his luncheon, when a tramp steals it; Charlie shrugs his shoulders, picks a handful of grass, peppers and salts it, and eats it with delicacy; then he pours water into a can, rinses the tips of his fingers as though in a finger bowl, and dries them on a rag – all performed with a restrained swagger.

This was followed by an Indian film – a costume piece derived from a traditional fairy-story. A kindly Indian next to us helped us with the plot, explaining, 'That is a bad man,' 'That is a elephant,' etc. When he wished to tell us that the hero had fallen in love with the heroine – a situation sufficiently apparent from their extravagant gestures of passion – he said, 'He wants to take her into the bushes.'

The church at Tabora was very beautiful; a great thatched barn, with low, whitewashed walls and rough wooden pillars daubed with the earth colour of the country. It was packed next day with a native congregation who sang at Mass with tremendous devotion. That afternoon I went for another drive with the bishop, and late in the evening caught the train for Kigoma.

SECOND NIGHTMARE

I arrived at Kigoma in the morning of February 2nd, a haphazard spatter of bungalows differing very little from the other lakeside stations I had passed through, except in the size and apparent disorder of its wharfs and goods yard. The lake steamers belong to the Belgian Chemin de Fer des Grands Lacs; notices everywhere are in French and Flemish; there are the offices of Belgian immigration authorities, vice-consulate, and customs; a huge unfinished building of the Congo trading company. But the impression that I had already left British soil was dissipated almost at once by the spectacle of a pair of Tanganyika policemen, who stood with the ticket collector at the station door and forcibly vaccinated the native passengers as they passed through.

It was now about noon and the heat was overpowering. I was anxious to get my luggage on board, but it had to be left at the customs sheds for examination when the official had finished his luncheon. A group of natives were squatting in the road, savages with filed teeth and long hair, very black, with broad shoulders and spindly legs, dressed in bits of skin and rag. A White Father of immense stature drove up in a box-body lorry containing crates, sacks, and nuns for trans-shipment; a red and wiry beard spread itself over his massive chest; clouds of dense, acrid smoke rose from his cheroot.

There was a little Greek restaurant in the main street, where I lunched and, after luncheon, sat on the verandah waiting for the customs office to open. A continual traffic of natives passed to and fro – most of them, in from the country, far less civilised than any I had seen since the Somalis; a few, in shirts, trousers, and hats, were obviously in European employment; one of them rode a bicycle and fell off it just in front of the restaurant; he looked very rueful when he got up, but when the passers-by laughed at him he began to laugh too and went off thoroughly pleased with himself as though he had made a good joke.

By about three I got my luggage clear, then after another long wait bought my ticket, and finally had my passport examined by British and Belgian officials. I was then able to go on board the *Duc de Brabant*. She was a shabby, wood-burning steamer, with passenger accommodation in the poop consisting of a stuffy little deck-saloon, with two or three cabins below and a padlocked lavatory. The short deck was largely taken up by the captain's quarters – an erection like a two-roomed bungalow, containing a brass double bed-stead with mosquito-curtains, numerous tables and chairs, cushions, photograph frames, mirrors, clocks, china and metal ornaments, greasy cretonnes and torn muslin, seedy little satin bows and ribbons, pots of dried grasses, pin-cushions, every conceivable sort of cheap and unseamanlike knick-knack. Clearly there was a woman on board. I found her knitting on the shady side of the deck-house. I asked her about cabins. She said her husband was asleep and was not to be disturbed until five. Gross snorting and grunting from the mosquito-curtains gave substance to her statement. There were three people asleep in the saloon. I went on shore again and visited the Congo agency, where I inquired about my aeroplane to Leopoldville. They were polite, but quite unhelpful. I must ask at Albertville.

Soon after five the captain appeared. No one, looking at him, would have connected him in any way with a ship; a very fat, very dirty man, a stained tunic open at his throat, unshaven, with a straggling moustache, crimson-faced, gummy-eyed, flat-footed. He would have seemed more at home as proprietor of an *estaminet*. A dozen or so passengers had now assembled – we were due to sail at six – and the captain lumbered round examining our tickets and passports. Every-one began claiming cabins. He would see to all that when we sailed, he said. When he came to me he said, 'Where is your medical certificate?'

I said I had not got one.

'It is forbidden to sail without a medical certificate.'

I explained that I had been given a visa, had bought a ticket, had had my passport examined twice by British and

Belgian officials, but that no one had said anything to me about a medical certificate.

'I regret it is forbidden to travel. You must get one.'

'But a certificate of what? What do you want certified?'

'It is no matter to me what is certified. You must find a doctor and get him to sign. Otherwise you cannot sail.'

This was three-quarters of an hour before the advertised time of departure. I hurried on shore and inquired where I could find a doctor. I was directed to a hospital some distance from the town, at the top of the hill. There were, of course, no taxis of any kind. I set out walking feverishly. Every now and then the steamer gave a whistle which set me going at a jog-trot for a few paces. At last, streaming with sweat, I reached the hospital. It turned out to be a club house; the hospital was about two miles away on the other side of the town. Another whistle from the *Duc de Brabant*. I pictured her sailing away across the lake with all my baggage, money, and credentials. I explained my difficulty to a native servant; he clearly did not at all understand what I wanted, but he caught the word doctor. I suppose he thought I was ill. Anyway, he lent me a boy to take me to a doctor's house. I set off again at high speed, to the disgust of my guide, and finally reached a bungalow where an Englishwoman was sitting in the garden with needlework and a book. No, her husband was not at home. Was it anything urgent?

I explained my predicament. She thought I might be able

to find him on the shore; he might be there at work on his speed-boat, or else he might be playing tennis, or perhaps he had taken the car out to Ujiji. I had better try the shore first.

Down the hill again, this time across country over a golf course and expanses of scrub. Sure enough, at one of the landing-stages about a quarter of a mile from the *Duc de Brabant*, I found two Englishmen fiddling with a motorboat. One of them was the doctor. I shouted down to him what I wanted. It took him some time to find any paper. In the end his friend gave him an old envelope. He sat down in the stern and wrote: '*I have examined Mr*' – 'What's your name?' – '*Waugh, and find him free from infectious disease, including omnis t.b. and trypansiniasis. He has been vaccinated.*' – 'Five shillings, please.'

I handed down the money; he handed up the certificate. That was that.

It was ten past six when I reached the *Duc de Brabant*, but she was still there. With a grateful heart I panted up the gangway and presented my certificate. When I had got my breath a little I explained to a sympathetic Greek the narrow escape I had had of being left behind. But I need not have hurried. It was a little after midnight before we sailed.

The boat was now very full. On our deck there were four or five Belgian officials and their wives, two mining engineers, and several Greek traders. There was also a plump young man with a pallid face and soft American voice. Unlike anyone I had seen for the past month, he wore a neat, dark suit, white collar and bow tie. He had a great deal of very neat luggage, including a typewriter and a bicycle. I offered him a drink and he said, 'Oh no, thank you,' in a tone which in four monosyllables contrived to express first surprise, then pain, then reproof, and finally forgiveness. Later I found that he was a member of the Seventh Day Adventist mission, on his way to audit accounts at Bulawayo.

The waist and forecastle were heaped with mail-bags and freight over which sprawled and scurried a medley of animals and native passengers. There were goats and calves and chickens, naked negro children, native soldiers, women suckling babies or carrying them slung between their shoulders, young girls with their hair plaited into pig-tails, which divided their scalps into symmetrical patches, girls with shaven pates and with hair caked in red mud, old negresses with bundles of bananas, over-dressed women with yellow and red cotton shawls and brass bangles, negro workmen in shorts, vests, and crumpled topis. There were several little stoves and innumerable pots of boiling banana. Bursts of singing and laughing.

They laid the tables in our saloon for dinner. We sat tightly packed at benches. There were three or four small children who were fed at the table. Two ragged servants cooked and served a very bad dinner. The captain collected the money. Presently he passed round a list of those to whom he had given cabins. I was not among them, nor was the American missionary nor any of the Greeks. We should have slipped him a tip with our tickets, I learned later. About a dozen of us were left without accommodation. Six wise men laid themselves out full length on the saloon benches immediately after dinner and established their claim for the night. The rest of us sat on our luggage on the deck. There were no seats or deck-chairs. Luckily it was a fine night, warm, unclouded, and windless. I spread an overcoat on the deck, placed a canvas grip under my head as a pillow and composed myself for sleep. The missionary found two little wooden chairs and sat stiff backed, wrapped in a rug, with his feet up supporting a book of Bible-stories on his knees. As we got up steam, brilliant showers of wood sparks rose from the funnel; soon after midnight we sailed into the lake; a gentle murmur of singing came from the bows. In a few minutes I was asleep.

I woke up suddenly an hour later and found myself shivering with cold. I stood up to put on my overcoat and immediately found myself thrown against the rail. At the same moment I saw the missionary's two chairs tip over sideways and him sprawl on the deck. A large pile of hand luggage upset and slid towards the side. There was a tinkle of broken china from the captain's quarters. All this co-incided with a torrential downpour of rain and a tearing wind. It was followed in a second or two by a blaze of light-ning and a shattering detonation. A chatter of alarm went up from the lower deck, and various protests of disturbed livestock. In the half-minute which it took us to collect our luggage and get into the saloon we were saturated with rain. And here we were in scarcely better conditions, for the windows, when raised, proved not to be of glass, but of wire gauze. The wind tore through them, water poured in and slopped from side to side. Women passengers came up squealing from their cabins below, with colourless, queasy faces. The saloon became intolerably overcrowded. We sat as we had at dinner, packed in rows round the two tables. The wind was so strong that it was impossible, single-handed, to open the door. Those who were ill – the American missionary was the first to go under – were obliged to remain in their places. The shriek of the wind was so loud that conversation was impossible; we just clung there, pitched and thrown, now out of our seats, now on top of one another; occasionally someone would fall asleep and wake up instantly with his head thumped hard against table or wall. It needed constant muscular effort to avoid injury. Vile retchings occurred on every side. Women whimpered at their husbands for support. The children yelled. We were all of us dripping and shivering. At last everyone grew quieter as alarm subsided and desperation took its place. They sat there, rigid and glum, gazing straight before them or supporting their heads in their hands until, a little before dawn, the wind dropped and rain ceased beating in; then some of them fell asleep, and others slunk back to their cabins. I went out on deck. It was still extremely cold, and the little boat bobbed and wallowed hopelessly in a heavy sea, but the storm was clearly over. Soon a green and silver dawn broke over the lake; it was misty all round us, and the orange sparks from the funnel were just visible against the whiter sky. The two stewards emerged with chattering teeth and attempted to set things to order in the saloon, dragging out rolls of sodden matting and swabbing up the waterlogged floor. Huddled groups on the lower deck began to disintegrate and a few cocks crowed; there was a clatter of breakfast cups and a welcome smell of coffee.

It was raining again before we reached harbour and moored against an unfinished concrete pier, where dripping convicts were working, chained together in gangs. Albertville was almost hidden in mist; a blur of white buildings against the obscurer background. Two rival hotel proprietors stood under umbrellas shouting for custom; one was Belgian, the other Greek. Officials came on board. We queued up and presented our papers one at a time. The inevitable questions: Why was I coming into the Congo? How much money had I? How long did I propose to stay there? Where was my medical certificate? The inevitable form to fill in – this time in duplicate: date and place of father's birth? Mother's maiden name? Maiden name of divorced wife? Habitual domicile? By this time I had learned not to reveal the uncertainty of my plans. I told them I was going direct to Matadi and was given a certificate of entry which I was to present to the immigration officer at the frontier. It took two hours before we were allowed to land.

Quite suddenly the rain stopped and the sun came out. Everything began to steam.

I spent two nights at Albertville. It consists of a single street of offices, shops, and bungalows. There are two hotels catering for visitors in transit to and from Tanganyika; no cinemas or places of amusement. There are white people serving in the shops, and white clerks at the railway station; no natives live in the town except a handful of dockers and domestic servants. The food at the hotel is fairly good; better than I have had for several weeks. The Belgian manager is amiable and honest. I spend my time making inquiries about the air service. No one knows anything about it. One thing is certain, that there has never been an air service at Albertville. They think there was one once at Kabalo; that there still may be. Anyway, there is a train to Kabalo the day after tomorrow. There is no alternative; one can either take the train to Kabalo or the boat back to Kigoma; there are no other means of communication in any direction. With some apprehension of coming discomfort, I purchase a ticket to Kabalo.

The train left at seven in the morning and made the journey in a little under eleven hours, counting a halt for luncheon at the wayside. It is an uneven line; so uneven that at times I was hardly able to read. I travelled first class to avoid the American missionary, and had the carriage to myself. For half the day it rained. The scenery was attractive at first; we pitched and rocked through a wooded valley with a background of distant hills, and later along the edge of a river broken by islands of vivid swamp. Towards midday, however, we came into bush country, featureless and dismal; there was no game to be seen, only occasional clouds of white butterflies; in the afternoon we jolted over mile upon mile of track cut through high grass, which grew right up on either side of the single line to the height of the carriages, completely shutting out all view, but mercifully shading us from the afternoon sun. There was a shower-bath attached to the first-class coach, an invaluable contribution to the comfort of a hot day's journey which might well be commended to the PLM. It was fantastic to discover, on a jolting single line in Central Africa, decencies which one cannot get on the Blue Train. It is perhaps fair to remark that the shower-bath was not, nor apparently had been for some time, in working order; but I have long ceased to hope for any railway carriage that will offer a tolerable water system. It seems to be well understood by coach designers in all parts of the world that the true measure of luxury consists in the number of unnecessary electric light switches and different coloured bulbs.

It was just before sundown when we reached Kabalo, a place of forbidding aspect. There was no platform; a heap of wood fuel and the abrupt termination of the line marked the station; there were other bits of line sprawling out to right and left; a few shabby trucks had been shunted on to one of these, and apparently abandoned; there were two or three goods sheds of corrugated iron and a dirty little canteen; apart from these, no evidence of habitation. In front of us lay the Upper Congo – at this stage of its course undistinguished among the great rivers of the world for any beauty or interest; a broad flow of water, bounded by swamps; since we were in the rainy season, it was swollen and brown. A barge or two lay in to the bank, and a paddle steamer, rusted all over, which was like a flooded Thames bungalow more than a ship. A bit of the bank opposite the railway-line had been buttressed up with concrete; on all sides lay rank swamp. Mercifully, night soon came on and hid this beastly place.

I hired a boy to sit on my luggage, and went into the canteen. There, through a haze of mosquitoes, I discerned a prominent advertisement of the Kabalo–Matadi air service; two or three railway officials were squatting about on stiff little chairs swilling tepid beer. There was a surly and dishevelled woman slopping round in bedroom slippers, with a tray of dirty glasses. In answer to my inquiry, she pointed out the patron, a torpid lump fanning himself in the only easy chair. I asked him when the next aeroplane left the coast; everyone stopped talking and stared at me when I put this question. The patron giggled. He did not know when the *next* would leave; the *last* went about ten months ago. There were only three ways of leaving Kabalo; either by train back to

Albertville or by river up or down stream. The *Prince Leopold* was due that evening for Bukama; in a day or so there would be a boat down the river; if I took that, I could, with judicious alternations of boat and rail, reach Matadi in under a month.

At this stage one of the railway officials interposed helpfully. There were trains from Bukama to a place called Port Francqui. If I wired, and if the wire ever reached its destination, I could arrange for the Elisabethville-Matadi air service to pick me up there. Failing that, I could get from Bukama on to the newly opened Benguela railway and come out on the coast at Lobita Bay in Portuguese West Africa. In any case, I had better go to Bukama. Kabalo, he remarked, was a dull place to stay in.

Two hours passed and there was no sign of the *Prince Leopold*. We ate a frightful (and very expensive) meal in the canteen. The Seventh Day Adventist came in from the railway-line, where he had been sitting in the dark to avoid the sight and smell of beer-drinking. He was travelling by the *Prince Leopold*, too. Another two hours and she arrived. We went on board that night and sailed at dawn.

The journey took four days. It was not uncomfortable. There was heavy rain half the time and the temperature was never insupportable. I had a cabin to myself, and I fought boredom, and to some extent overcame it, by the desperate expedient of writing – it was there, in fact, that I ground out the first two chapters of this book.

The *Prince Leopold* was a large paddle-steamer, twice the size of the *Rusinga*, with half the staff. The captain and a Greek steward seemed to do all the work; the former young and neurotic, the latter middle-aged and imperturbable, both very grubby. It was a great contrast to all those dapper bachelors on Lake Victoria, with their white collars and changes of uniform. The captain had married quarters in the top storey (one could only regard it as a floating house, not as a ship); his strip of deck was fringed with pots of ferns and palm; below him was the European passengers' deck, two rows of tiny cabins, an observation platform, and a bath-room; the ground floor was occupied by cargo and native passengers. We stopped two or three times a day at desolate little stations, where a crowd of natives and two sickly Belgian agents would come down to greet us. Sometimes there was a native village; usually nothing except a single shed and a pile of timber. We delivered mail, took up cargo, and occasionally effected some change of passengers. These were all Greek or Belgian; either traders or officials; except for the inevitable round of handshaking each morning there was very little intercourse. The Seventh Day Adventist became slightly ill; he attributed his discomfort to the weakness of the tea. The scenery was utterly dreary. Flat papyrus-swamps on either side broken by rare belts of palm. The captain employed his time in inflicting slight wounds on passing antelope with a miniature rifle. Occasionally he would be convinced that he had killed something; the boat would stop and all the native passengers disembark and scramble up the side with loud whoops and yodels. There was difficulty in getting them back. The captain would watch them, through binoculars, plunging and gambolling about in the high grass; at first he would take an interest in the quest, shouting directions to them; then he would grow impatient and summon them back; they would disappear further and further, thoroughly enjoying their romp. He would have the siren sounded for them – blast after blast. Eventually they would come back, jolly, chattering, and invariably empty-handed.

We were due to arrive at Bukama on Sunday (February 8th). The train for Port Francqui did not leave until the following Tuesday night. It was customary for passengers to wait on board, an arrangement that was profitable to the company and comparatively comfortable for them. I was prevented from doing this by a violent and inglorious altercation with the captain, which occurred quite unexpectedly on the last afternoon of the journey.

I was sitting in my cabin, engrossed in the affairs of Abyssinia, when the captain popped in and, with wild eye and confused speech, demanded to be shown the ticket for my motor-bicycle. I am convinced that he was sober, but I am less sure of his sanity. I replied that I had no motor-bicycle. 'What, no motor-bicycle?' 'No, no motor-bicycle.' He shook his head, clicked his tongue and popped out again. I went on writing.

In half an hour he was back again; this time with a fellow passenger who spoke English.

'The captain wishes me to tell you that he must see the ticket for your motor-bicycle.'

'But I have already told the captain that I have no motor-bicycle.'

'You do not understand. It is necessary to have a ticket for a motor-bicycle.'

'I have no motor-bicycle.'

They left me again.

Ten minutes later the captain was back. 'Will you kindly show me your motor-bicycle.'

'I have no motor-bicycle.'

'It is on my list that you have a motor-bicycle. Will you kindly show it to me.'

'I have no motor-bicycle.'

'But it is on my list.'

'I am sorry. I have no motor-bicycle.'

Again he went away; again he returned; now, beyond question, stark crazy. 'The motor-bicycle – the motor-bicycle! I must see the motor-bicycle.'

'I have no motor-bicycle.'

It is idle to pretend that I maintained a dignified calm. I was in a tearing rage, too. After all we were in the heart of the tropics where tempers are notoriously volatile.

'Very well, I will search your luggage. Show it to me.'

'It is in this cabin. Two suitcases under the bunk; one bag on the rack.'

'Show it to me.'

'Look for it yourself.' As I say, an inglorious schoolboy brawl.

'I am the captain of this ship. Do you expect me to move luggage?'

'I am a passenger. Do you expect me to?'

He went to the door and roared for a boy. No one came. With a trembling hand I attempted to write. He roared again. Again. At last a sleepy boy ambled up. 'Take those suitcases from under the bunk.'

I pretended to be writing. I could hear the captain puffing just behind me (it was a very small cabin).

'Well,' I said, 'have you found a motor-bicycle?'

'Sir, that is my affair,' said the captain.

He went away. I thought I had heard the last of the incident. In half an hour he was back. 'Pack your bag. Pack your bag instantly.'

'But I am staying on board until Tuesday.'

'You are leaving at once. I am the captain. I will not allow people of your kind to stay here another hour.'

In this way I found myself stranded on the wharf at Bukama with two days to wait for my train. A humiliating situation, embittered by the Seventh Day Adventist, who came to offer his sympathy. 'It doesn't do to argue,' he said, 'unless you understand the language.' Damn him.

I thought I had touched bottom at Kabalo, but Bukama has it heavily beaten. If ever a place merited the epithet 'God-forsaken' in its literal sense, it is that station. An iron bridge spans the river leading from the European quarter to the desolated huts of the native navvies who built it. Two ruined bungalows stand by the waterside and the overgrown Government rest-house, whose use has been superseded by the *Prince Leopold*; it is still nominally open, and it was here that I should have to stay if I decided to wait for the Port Francqui train. It is unfurnished and, presumably, infested with spirillum tick. Some distance from the landing-point lies the jumble of huts that serve as ticket and goods office of the Katanga railway. A road leads up the hill, where there are two abandoned offices and a Greek bar and general store. At the top of the hill is the administrative part – a flag-staff, the bungalow of the resident official, and a small hospital round which squatted a group of dejected patients enveloped in bandages. A platoon of native soldiers shuffled past. The heat and damp were appalling, far worse than anything I had met in Zanzibar. At sundown, swarms of soundless, malarial mosquitoes appeared. I sat in the Greek bar, with sweat splashing down like rain-water from my face to the floor; the proprietor knew only a few words of French. In these few words he advised me to leave Bukama as soon as I could, before I went down with fever. He himself was ashen and shivering from a recent bout. There was a train some time that evening for Elisabethville. I decided to take it. The Seventh Day Adventist, I found, was travelling with me.

We had a long wait, for no one knew the time when the train was expected. The station was completely dark except for one window at which a vastly bearded old man sold the tickets. Little groups of natives sat about on the ground. Some of them carried lanterns, some had lighted little wood fires and were cooking food. There was a ceaseless drumming in the crowd – as difficult to locate as the song of a grasshopper – and now and again a burst of low singing. At ten o'clock the train came in. The carriage was full of mosquitoes; there was no netting; the windows were jammed; the seats hard and extremely narrow. Two Greeks ate oranges all through the night. In this way I went to Elisabethville.

Elisabethville has really no part in this Nightmare. The two days I spent there were placid and wholly agreeable. I arrived early in the afternoon on the day after my departure from Bukama and stayed there until late on the Wednesday evening. I lived in an hotel kept by an ex-officer with a fine cavalry moustache. There was decent wine, good cigars, and very good food. There was a large, cool room in which to work, and a clean bath-room; in the town I found a bookshop and an excellent cinema. The only nightmarish thing was the disorganisation of my plans – but these had been so frequently changed during the past month that I had ceased to put any trust in their permanence.

The air service proved definitely and finally to be useless to me. There was, it is true, some prospect of an aeroplane leaving for the coast during the next week or two, provided that enough passengers demanded it. Since the fare was slightly in excess of that charged by Imperial Airways for the whole journey from London to Cape Town, it seemed to me unlikely that there would be much custom. The 'newly opened' railway to Lobita Bay was closed again. It had only been possible in the dry season when motor-transport could bridge the unfinished gap at the Belgian end of the line. I could return to Bukama and go to the coast via Port Francqui and Leopoldville, catching a Belgian steamer at Boma; but, paradoxically enough, the quickest way to Europe – and by this time I was hard in the grip of travel-phobia – was hundreds of miles out of the way through the Rhodesias and the Union of South Africa. There I could get a fast mail-boat from Cape Town to Southampton. The journey had already vastly exceeded my original estimate and I was uncomfortably short of money;[1] accordingly I decided to follow this route.

I had some difficulty in explaining, to the satisfaction of the

1. Since expenses are always an important part of travel, it may be of interest to remark that, from the date I left England in October 1930,

immigration officer whose permission was necessary before
I could leave the Congo, why I diverged so much from the itin-
erary outlined in my certificate of entry. In the end, however,
he understood my difficulties and gave me leave to depart. In
the meantime I worked, rested, and enjoyed the comfort and
tranquillity of Elisabethville. How reassuring are these occasional reconciliations with luxury. How often in Europe, after
too much good living, I have begun to doubt whether the
whole business of civilised taste is not a fraud put upon us by
shops and restaurants. Then, after a few weeks of gross, colonial
wines, hard beds, gritty bath-water, awkward and surly subordinates, cigars from savage Borneo or the pious Philippines,
cramped and unclean quarters, and tinned foodstuffs, one
realises that the soft things of Europe are not merely rarities
which one has been taught to prefer because they are expensive, but thoroughly satisfactory compensations for the rough
and tumble of earning one's living – and a far from negligible
consolation for some of the assaults and deceptions by which
civilisation seeks to rectify the balance of good fortune.

Six days in the train with little to relieve the monotony. At
Bulawayo I bought a novel called *A Muster of Vultures*, in which

---

until my return in March 1931, the total cost of my journey, including
a good many purchases of tropical clothes, local painting, carving,
etc., and consistent losses at all games of skill and chance, came to a
little short of £500.

287

the villain burned away his victims' faces with 'the juice of a tropical cactus'; at Mafeking I bought peaches; once our windows were bedewed with spray from the Victoria Falls; once everything was powdered deep in dust from the great Karoo Desert; once we took in a crowd of desperate men dismissed from the Rhodesian copper mines; two were known to be without tickets or passports and there was a frantic search for them by bare-kneed police officers, up and down the corridors and under the seats; one of them stole nine shillings from the half-caste boy who made up the beds. When we changed on to a new train at Bulawayo there were white stewards in the dining-car; after so many months it seemed odd and slightly indecent to see white men waiting on each other. Currency consisted chiefly of threepenny bits (called 'tickies') and gold sovereigns; also of a variety of notes issued by different banking corporations.

At last we arrived in Cape Town; a hideous city that reminded me of Glasgow; trams running between great stone offices built in Victorian Gothic; one or two gracious relics of the eighteenth century; down-at-heel negroes and half-castes working in the streets; dapper Jews in the shops.

I had about forty pounds left in my pocket. A boat was sailing that afternoon. I could either wire to London for more money and await its arrival or I could take a third-class ticket home. I left that day. For £20 I bought a berth in a large and clean cabin. There were two other occupants; one a delightful man from North Devon who had been working on the railway; the other a Jew boy from a shop. The stewards treated us with superiority, but good nature; the food was like that of an exceptionally good private school – large luncheons, substantial meat teas, biscuit suppers. There was a very fat Welsh clergyman travelling in the third class with us. His congregation came to see him off. They sang hymns on the quayside, which he conducted with extravagant waving of his arms until we were out of earshot. Chiefly they sang one whose refrain was 'I'm sailing home', but they had been a little deluded by the felicity of these words, for the general theme of the composition was less appropriate. It referred, in fact, not to the journey from Cape Town to England, but to death and the return of the soul to its Creator. However, no one seemed depressed by this prediction, and the clergyman's wife sang it with great feeling long after her husband had stopped beating the time.

It was a pleasant voyage. In the evenings we played 'pontoon', a simplified form of *vingt-et-un*, a game which in itself is far from complex. In the mornings we boxed or played 'pontoon'. There were frequent sing-songs, led by a troop of disgruntled dirt-track racers whose season in South Africa had been a failure.

We stopped at St Helena, where I should not the least object to being exiled, and at Tenerife, where everyone bought very foul cigars. A day later, however, we ran into rough and very cold weather and the cigar-smoking fell off noticeably. There were heavy seas for the rest of the voyage, and most of the women remained below. A sports committee was organised, and proved the occasion for much bad blood; the Welsh clergyman in particular came in for criticism, on the ground that a man with a child of his own had no business to organise the children's fancy-dress party. 'He'll give his own little boy the best prize,' they said. 'Who wouldn't?' He replied by saying that he would have them know that, when he came out, a special presentation had been made to him by his fellow passengers in thanks for his public-spirited management of the deck-games. They said, 'That's as may be.' He said he would sooner give up the whole thing than have his honour questioned. It was all most enjoyable.

Eventually, on March 10th, we berthed at Southampton.

THIRD NIGHTMARE

On the night of my return I dined in London. After dinner we were in some doubt where to go. The names I suggested had long ceased to be popular. Eventually we decided, and drove to a recently opened supper-restaurant which, they said, was rather amusing at the moment.

It was underground. We stepped down into the blare of noise as into a hot swimming-pool, and immersed ourselves; the atmosphere caught our breath like the emanation in a brewery over the tanks where fermentation begins. Cigarette-smoke stung the eyes.

A waiter beckoned us to a small table, tight-packed among other tables, so that our chairs rubbed backs with their neighbours. Waiters elbowed their way in and out, muttering abuse in each other's ears. Some familiar faces leered through the haze; familiar voices shrilled above the din.

We chose some wine.

'You'll have to take something to eat with it.'

We ordered seven-and-sixpenny sandwiches.

Nothing came.

A negro in fine evening clothes was at the piano, singing.

Afterwards, when he went away, people fluttered their hands at him and tried to catch his eye. He bestowed a few patronising nods. Someone yelled, 'He's losing his figure.'

A waiter came and said, 'Any more orders for drinks before closing time?' We said we had had nothing yet. He made a face and pinched another waiter viciously in the arm, pointing at our table and whispering in Italian. That waiter pinched another. Eventually the last-pinched waiter brought a bottle and slopped out some wine into glasses. It frothed up and spilt on the tablecloth. We looked at the label and found that it was not the wine we had ordered.

Someone shrilled in my ear: 'Why, Evelyn, where *have* you been? I haven't seen you about anywhere for days.'

My friends talked about the rupture of an engagement which I did not know was contracted.

The wine tasted like salt and soda-water. Mercifully a waiter whisked it away before we had time to drink it. 'Time, if you please.'

I was back in the centre of the Empire, and in the spot where, at the moment, 'everyone' was going. Next day the gossip-writers would chronicle the young MPs, peers, and financial magnates who were assembled in that rowdy cellar, hotter than Zanzibar, noiser than the market at Harar, more reckless of the decencies of hospitality than the taverns of Kabalo or Tabora. And a month later the wives of English officials would read about it, and stare out across the bush or jungle or desert or forest or golf links, and envy their sisters at home, and wish they had the money to marry rich men.

Why go abroad?

See England first.

Just watch London knock spots off the Dark Continent.

I paid the bill in yellow African gold. It seemed just tribute from the weaker races to their mentors.